To my old pal,

Peter Megargee Brown.

with admiration and

affection —

Walter J P Cauley Jr

Christmas 1973

MONARCHS-IN-WAITING

MONARCHS-IN-WAITING

WALTER J. P. CURLEY, JR.

ILLUSTRATED WITH PHOTOGRAPHS AND MAPS

DODD, MEAD & COMPANY
NEW YORK

ISBN: 0-396-06840-5
Library of Congress Catalog Card Number: 73-11549

Printed in the United States of America
by The Cornwall Press, Inc., Cornwall, N. Y.

FOR TAITSIE

ACKNOWLEDGMENTS

I am very grateful to the claimants themselves for their spirit of cooperation. Virtually all the claimants responded with (varying degrees of) assistance. From indirect intelligence and a sympathetic assumption, I ascribe the minor exceptions to the pressure of personal situations. As in most matters of life, the bigger the man the more generous was the response. None of the claimants raised objections. My thanks go to all of them.

A particularly warm appreciation resulted from the encounters with Archduke Otto of Habsburg, Crown Prince Louis-Ferdinand of Germany, dom Duarte of Portugal, and don Juan of Spain, whose candor and hospitality were so genuine in the interviews.

Special indebtedness is due to my good friend Ian Finlay of Dublin, a free-lance photojournalist who visited various claimants in the winter of 1972. With degrees in history and political science from Irish and German universities, experience as a critic and broadcaster for the BBC, and a well-peeled photographer's eye, Ian Finlay is a totally contemporary man who is able to perceive some current relevance to the claimants and their positions without awe or sentiment.

For their help, information, and support in many other different ways I am also very grateful to the following: Mr. Louis S. Auchincloss, New York; Mr. Ivan Bilibin, Reading, Berkshire,

England; Lt. Col. Julian C. du Parc Braham, London; Miss T. Colebrook, Madrid; Mr. F. Garcin, Paris; Colonel George I. Guentcheff, Madrid; Mrs. Letitia Baldrige Hollensteiner, New York; Anne Lady Inchiquin, Newmarket-on-Fergus, Clare, Ireland; Allen T. Klots, Jr., New York; Mr. James P. McGarry, Collooney, Sligo, Ireland; Colonel José A. deLaCour Macia, Estoril; Mr. Edward MacLysaught, Dublin, Ireland; Count/Judge Juvenal Marchisio, New York; Mrs. Lydwine Petrie, Bonn; Mr. Bernard Picot, Paris; Baron Michael Raben, Wicklow, Ireland; Mr. David Ryus, New York; Miss Vivian Spaulding, New York; Mr. Peter Stephaich, Paris; and Mr. Eduardo S. de Vicuna, Madrid.

I devote all my attentions to improving the welfare of my subjects, since I wish to save my soul and go to Heaven.

—King Charles III of Spain (1750)

I forgive with all my heart those who have become my enemies without my having given them any reasons for so doing, and I pray God to forgive them, as well as those who, through a false or misconceived zeal, have done me much evil.

—From the Will of King Louis XVI of France before his Execution. (1793)

The best reason why monarchy is a strong government is that it is an intelligible government. The mass of mankind understand it, and they hardly anywhere in the world understand any other.

—Walter Bagehot
Political Writer (1826–1877)

Nothing under the sun would induce me to accept a Kingdom. A crown is too heavy a thing to be put on lightly. It has to be worn by those born to that destiny, but that any man should willingly take on the responsibility, not being constrained by duty to do so, passes my comprehension.

—H.R.H. Prince Christopher of Greece (1888–1940)

If a nation does not want a monarchy, change the nation's mind. If a nation does not need a monarchy, change the nation's needs.

—Jan Christian Smuts
Minister of South Africa
(1939–1948)

Monarchy is the most ancient form of government still in use although, as practiced in the West, it is but an atavistic symbol of human continuity. Yet whether as observed in Europe where sovereigns only reign or in Asia or Africa where they so often rule, the profession of kingship has one cardinal rule: It is a lifetime job. The crown is almost never relinquished by its wearer except after violent cataclysms, most frequently war or revolution. Edward VIII of England was a singular exception. He resigned the world's most prestigious crown because of love.

—C. L. Sulzberger
Foreign Affairs, New York Times
(May 1972)

INTRODUCTION

This book is basically about kings—not dead ones, but live and valid royal persons who are among us today. They are sovereigns who are awaiting a return of their sovereignty. They are all European and there are eighteen of them.[1] They are monarchs without crowns.

I have attempted to present a current look at each of these shadow sovereigns, and to deal with the *claim* of this small, cohesive, and very special group of people *to the government of Europe*. The legitimacy of the claim withstands some rigorous buffeting. The claim became more impressive to me the more I learned about it.

As an American commoner, tried and true, any monarchist concept seemed to me, at best, specious. I was, however, fascinated by the fact that some people in this wild world took very seriously the fact of hereditary governmental legitimacy.

Over a period of years, as I encountered ersatz titles, café society princelings, and the regiments of types in the United States and Europe who are titillated by noblesse, I rediscovered the fact that what keeps those things alive is an honest-to-God group of people who have a *right*. They have kept to themselves; they have, in the main, protected their legitimacy. With few exceptions, they have lived and bred in the terribly stringent tradition of their claim.

This book is about these claimants.

There were several temptations about what sort of slant this book would take. One was to treat the entire subject of royal claimants in a frivolous fashion—point out how ridiculous their posture was in today's world. Another was to treat it academically —make it another summary of history. And another was to turn it into a social guide to Europe. What follows is, inadvertently, probably an amalgam of many things, including some of these.

What this book is not is a put-down, a gossip-mongering chronicle, or merely a recitation of celebrities.

At the concept of this book, my tongue was firmly in my cheek. As it progressed, my admiration for the claimants increased, and the tenor of the book changed. The book has been written with no bulging cheek nor dazzled eyes.

Several avid royalty-watchers told me at the outset of the book that the eighteen claimants were exceedingly private people who would not agree to any personal contact—interviews, questionnaires, and so forth. To the contrary, of the current royal claimants, only one chose not to respond to an approach.

But more of these minutiae in what comes. This can be a reference book, or a walk through a very old looking glass. Please know, however, one thing: The claimants are *real* people. Some of them have also a remotely prospective hand on a tiller which may guide Europe in the next thousand years. They certainly shaped it over the last thousand years. Indeed, they owned it. Maybe they still do—*de jure*. And would it be so bad if they did?

With great pleasure laced with substantial admiration for the subjects, I present a republican view of a royalist situation: a primer for the unabashed royalty-watcher.

W.J.P.C.

NOTES

1. As this book was going to press, the eighteenth royal person joined the ranks of claimants—King Constantine of Greece. See page 207.

CONTENTS

PART ONE

Reflections in an Ancient Glass

I went to a dinner party in New York City several years ago at the house of a rather prominent social lioness. There were twenty people. One of the guests was a direct descendant of Thomas Jefferson, a vibrant, engaging man in his middle forties. Another guest was a taciturn Italian count with arthritis, bad breath, and an obscure name previously unfamiliar to everyone present with the exception of the hostess. Most of the women gravitated competitively toward the count, and literally collided with each other for his attention. The Jeffersonian mystique carried no magic. An old phenomenon was at work: Americans, for paradoxical reasons, have always been fascinated by nobility.[1]

The mere mention of a title seems to conjure up in the minds of many people a collage of images redundant with villas, castles, palaces, coronets, candlelit balls, liveried servants, power politics, romantic and profane love, jewels and gold, fast cars, and impeccable manners. Even if the bearer of the title merely hustled stocks and bonds on commission—as many do—and had not lived in his "homeland" for several generations, the visions in the eyes of the beholders are generally undaunted.

Americans, however, are not the only ones to palpitate over the allure of a noble name. Many Europeans play the game of noble-watching with even more fervor. The social cachet of a title is understood more fully, and indeed, respected in varying degrees. The most highly developed version of the game, and ultimately the most entrancing, is that of *royalty-watching*. And here reality and fantasy blend together to create a truly compelling fascination for a great many people in the world.

While kingdoms and empires, principalities and dukedoms seem gilded memories of the past, the fact is, however, that in Europe alone there remain today nine royal and reigning families: the kingdoms of Belgium, Denmark, Great Britain, Norway, Holland, and Sweden; the principalities of Liechtenstein and Monaco; and the grand duchy of Luxembourg.

The situation in Spain has had the effect of catalyzing some fantasy into some reality: When General Franco assumed control almost thirty-five years ago and abolished the short-lived republic, he returned Spain constitutionally to a monarchy—without a king. Two years ago Prince Juan-Carlos, grandson of the last Spanish king, was designated by Franco to assume the crown in the next few years. This development has not only been a boon to the game of noble-watching but has given a remote tingle of hope to some of the disenfranchised royalty themselves.

Of great and continuing interest to royalty-watchers have been the kings in exile—the claimants and pretenders to the various thrones. (In brief, a claimant possesses a recognized legitimate dynastic right to the crown should the previous royal house be restored; a pretender is a claimant whose just title to the throne may be disputed by reason of rival claims by another of the same royal house.) Some of these exiles still harbor a hope of a return to the throne, and these hopes, no matter how dim, have received some encouragement by both the circumstances in Spain, and the hard fact of the enduring monarchies.

There are, therefore, a number of claimants to various thrones who are interesting historically, and in many cases, personally and politically. These individuals are among us today. They belong to families who, by their strength, intelligence, culture, intrigue, and power, have constructed Europe over the past thousand years. With a proper roll of the dice some of them might get the family jobs back. In the meantime, these kings-without-thrones treasure their claims, muse over the past, and wonder about the future.

Is it absolutely ridiculous to consider that there might be some merit to a return of the monarchy to certain countries? My first reaction would have been: Yes, ridiculous. But, if one considered each claimant as a person, as a candidate for political office, as an individual of accomplishment or at least prospectively so, the claimants emerge, not as anachronisms or vestigial structures, but as cultured, educated, serious people whose assets could be turned to their homelands' use.

They are, for the most part, internationalists by heritage and education. They speak several languages fluently; they are related and on familiar terms with each other; they are well versed in their countries' histories, current politics, and economics; they are philosophical; and they have had time to see the mistakes, indulgences, and weaknesses of the monarchies that toppled—including their own.

The claimants have had the discipline and the concern to impose—in most cases—strictures and rules that serve to keep their legitimacy alive. They have studied; they have made a family point of remaining aloof from the blandishments of the social circuit; they have married people with bloodlines compatible with the heritage. They have literally run their lives in a *noblesse oblige* tradition, with the essential difference that, in their cases, it is the compelling *royauté oblige* tradition.

Among the claimants dealt with in this book there is not one that is a public gossip item, a newsworthy playboy, a known fool.

There are none that are not distinguished, private people trying to make their way in the same world as we do with the added responsibility of trying to keep their dynastic traditions legitimate.

The general view is that royal personages live off money and treasures that the family had siphoned from the treasuries over the generations. Even if the cash is gone, we have the sneaking feeling that should the princess need a new pair of shoes, a villa, or some money to play the stockmarket, she has only to sell a diadem or a tiara. There is some truth to this. Certain family members of the monarchs-in-waiting have sold gems, furniture, paintings—but just like anyone else. And usually to buy groceries, pay school bills, or have the roof fixed. Mainly, however, they are persons living decently on money the family had invested over the years, money provided by donations from a dwindling falange of monarchist sympathizers, and money earned by their own efforts. Some, of course, married royal or noble spouses who have similar sources of income, and in some cases, spouses who have a great deal of money.

The community of claimants—if such a phrase is possible—is not unlike any other. There are poor, comfortable, and rich ones. There are bright ones and average ones. There are also dummies. But, taken as a group, by most standards they are solid thoroughbreds with all the strengths and weaknesses that the term implies. They have accomplished, however, a major feat by keeping their claims alive—if only in their own minds and in their styles of life. They remain ready to serve. Many are eminently able to serve their countries.

In the autumn of 1947 I was in Paris; I had come down slowly from Scandinavia by boat, bicycle, train, and foot, and had not been impressed by the general atmosphere of panic that some American political observers seemed to detect in the countries of

Continental Europe. To be sure, there were the eternal discussions about "the Government" in each country, and often tense predictions regarding Soviet Russia's intentions. The general topic of communism always drew participants. But there was no seething turmoil—just fatigue, ennui, and a spontaneous enthusiasm for recalling the halcyon years of the past.

The exact dates of "the Good Old Days" varied with the individual's age and nationality. A mean average of nostalgia would place the era roughly between 1880 and 1930. I often chided my European friends for remembering too well a colorful and lusty past that bore no realistic relationship to the present or future. I was, at last, amazed to find in Paris a body of practical and intelligent sophisticates who firmly believed that this general continental nostalgia had latent political power which would, in the next decade, become most articulate. In France this group is known as the Monarchists.

Before leaving Paris, I had lunch with the former Princess de F. − − L. in her "hotel" in Faubourg St. Germain. Among the eleven other guests there were three men in the Chamber of Deputies, the ex-consul general from Peking (who had been elevated to a responsible post in the French Ministry for Foreign Affairs), the son of an English peer, two gentlemen engaged in commerce, and four noble Frenchwomen. In their discussion of everyday politics, the cost of living, international trade, and so forth, there was a complete absence of naïveté or impractical idealism. They shared, however, a belief in the real possibility (and among the more fervent, the probability) of the return of a monarch to the throne of France.

Even in the heady atmosphere of the princess's apartments I could not suppress an attitude of derision at such a blatantly anachronistic belief in the future trend of French politics. The princess herself stated, however, on "unassailable authority," that the

Count of Paris, the present claimant to the throne of France, had had "unofficial discussions with a notable British statesman in the Spring of 1947" (Winston Churchill) and had come away with the impression that the success of a royalist resurgence in France would not be received unsympathetically by a Conservative government in England.

Great stress was made, during our discussions, on the evasive quality of "legitimacy" in the government. The legitimate claim of the monarchist movement, they felt, reached the understanding, emotions, and pride of the people, even though, in France, the days of the last monarch were relegated to the early memories of the average Frenchman's grandfather.

It was felt, moreover, that a monarchy (if limited and constitutional, along the lines enjoyed by the British) eminently suited the French, and general European, mentality. They agreed that the violent expulsion of the past French monarchies was in keeping with the democratic trend of the times—but that the rancor of the French people had been directed against the *individuals* (including the monarch himself) who had misused the institution of monarchy, rather than against the basic principles of the monarchial system. It was unfortunate, they felt, that the passionate opposition of the people to certain abuses had resulted in "uprooting the entire tree rather than pruning the diseased limbs." England, they cited, had similarly purged their government of individuals in past history, but the thought of dissolving the *principle* of monarchy was, as it is today, repugnant to the majority of Englishmen in all walks of life. The Princess de F. — — L. and her colleagues believed that many European nations, faced with the vacuum created by a violently uprooted "legitimate" (if misguided) hereditary government, had turned too eagerly to the substitute despotism epitomized by the national socialism of Hitler, the fascism of Mussolini, or the Soviet communism of Stalin.

The reasoning that, I noted, supported the French monarchist sincerity and hope for the future drew a measure of its strength from such principles as a nation's need for governmental continuity or "legitimacy," the people's pride in its hereditary representative, the moral responsibilty of a family, or individual thereof, devoted exclusively from birth to the service of the country, and the simple but often effective expedient of marriage and rapport between royal houses to knit diplomatic relations. The French Monarchists admit the absolute necessity for a representative government wherein the wishes of the people may be legally expressed by voting. But they feel that this democratic procedure should, and will again, be supplemented by a constitutional royal house. (Most of the modern French Monarchists tacitly endorse the abolition of ennobled aristocracy; that is, they feel the restoration of the *royal* house is necessary—without regalvanizing the socially inequitable structure of nobility. This enlightened system is seen today in Norway, for example.)

Before returning to America I talked to French butchers, automobile makers, and farmers on the subject and was not a little surprised to note a favorable—if lethargic and amused—reaction to the monarchist or royalist movement. They felt generally that it would be "nice" to have a king again; they wanted no return of the pointless pomp and let-them-eat-cake absolutism of the past, but they felt that a royal house would draw the people together more firmly—like a human flag. They would fight to the death for the vote and the right of the people to fire undesirable representatives; but I noticed that their imaginations were piqued by the idea of a French king, constitutionally limited. A great point of interest to me was that the average man's thought automatically went to the Count of Paris (or, in some cases, to Prince Louis-Napoleon) as the logical man for the resumption of the monarchy.

They wanted no newly created sovereign; they unconsciously recognized the existence of the "claim" of the royal family and thereby gave some credence to the logic of legitimacy.

It occurred to me that a movement, *properly guided and campaigned,* for the return of a limited French monarchy would, in the present day of incipient chaos, possibly be received by an astounding degree of favor from the people themselves.

Stimulated by this hypothesis regarding France, I subsequently discussed the analagous situation, over a period of years in many parts of the world, with different types of Germans, Austrians, Italians, Spaniards, Portuguese, and exiled Hungarians, Rumanians, Bulgarians, Albanians, Yugoslavs, and Russians. In all the countries represented by these nationalities, there exists today a legitimate claimant to their various thrones.

In discussions with some men and women who had originated in countries currently behind the Iron Curtain, I noted a markedly favorable feeling regarding the bona fide claims of their exiled monarchs. My informants were not predominantly titled gentlemen who hoped, in comic-opera style, for a return of their king and castle. They dispassionately credited the monarchist sentiment with having a latent political force among the people—if the yoke of communism could be removed and such a sentiment be given free expression.

The royalist or monarchist faction in Spain is no longer a movement; it is the hard fact. The king has been designated, and a return of the monarch to the throne is, at this moment, assured. The Portuguese sentiment and the possibility of a return to sovereignty of their royal house lie somewhere between the renascent French monarchist political stirrings and the almost accomplished plans of the Spanish royalist party.

The Italian monarchists were definitely back in the game about twenty years ago. In the 1952 elections, the rapidly rising Fascist party, the Italian social movement (MSI) teamed with the Italian Monarchist party and captured both the provincial and city councils of Naples and Bari. In Rome, where the Christian Democrats' majority bloc dominated, the Neo-Fascist-Monarchist alliance showed a gain of a hundred and fifty thousand votes over the 1948 balloting and soared from 4.7 percent of the Italian's total vote in 1950 to 21.3 percent that year. Achille Lauro, president of the Italian Monarchist party, telegraphed the exiled Italian king in Portugal as follows: "The great victory in Naples and Southern Italy has opened a sure road to victory . . . we shall continue in the assurance, now already well founded, that we shall restore to Italy, by democratic means, her King." The 1953 elections in Italy again placed the Monarchists in a crucial, if minor, position in the government. Italian politics in 1972 were again in turmoil. Strange turns of events could take place that might provide the spark which the Monarchists seek.

Call it nostalgia or castles in the air, there are stirrings—some now imperceptible, as in most of the Iron Curtain countries, and some notably articulate, as in Spain—which may conceivably change the political picture in Europe in the coming decades.

NOTES

1. Some Americans caress the thought that the Father of His Country and the British sovereign are directly related. George Washington's great-grandfather was also Queen Elizabeth II's great-great-great-great-great-great-great-grandfather. *See* The American Monarchial Connection, p. 219.

PART TWO

The Claimants

Who are the claimants and exiled monarchs dreaming of the day when they can dust off their crowns and return to their legitimate sovereignties? *Where* are they, and *what* are they doing? Remember their names; you may well hear of some of them again—or, at the very least, a closer look at them will provide a definite advantage in the old game of royalty-watching.

The people of whom we speak are:

Albania	His Majesty King Leka I
Austria-Hungary	His Imperial and Royal Highness Archduke Otto of Austria and King of Hungary
Bulgaria	His Majesty King Simeon II
France	1) His Royal Highness, Monseigneur Henri d'Orléans, Count of Paris 2) His Imperial Highness, Prince Louis Napoleon Bonaparte
Germany	His Imperial and Royal Highness Prince Louis-Ferdinand of Prussia
Greece	His Majesty King Constantine II, King of Greece, Prince of Denmark (*see* Appendix C)
Ireland	1) The O'Conor don, the Reverend Charles Denis Mary Joseph Anthony O'Conor 2) Sir Phaedrig Lucius Ambrose O'Brien, Lord Inchiquin

	3) Fourth Baron O'Neill, Lord Raymond Arthur Clanaboy O'Neill
Italy	His Majesty King Umberto II
Portugal	His Royal Highness dom Duarte Nuño, Duke of Braganza
Rumania	His Majesty King Michael I
Russia	His Imperial Highness Grand Duke Vladimir
Spain	1) His Royal Highness don Juan de Bourbon et Battenberg
	2) His Royal Highness don Juan-Carlos de Bourbon et Battenberg
Turkey	His Imperial Highness Prince Osman Fuad
Yugoslavia	His Royal Highness Prince Alexander

King Zog and new Queen Geraldine after wedding in Tirana, Albania, 1938. (*New York Herald Tribune*)

ALBANIA

Zog and Geraldine at parade celebrating 10th Anniversary of his reign. Durazzo, 1939. (*New York Herald Tribune*)

RIGHT: The Albanian King and Queen in exile. London, 1940. (*New York Herald Tribune*)

The late King Zog, his Queen Geraldine, and Prince (now King) Leka on his 13th birthday. Alexandria, Egypt, 1952. (*New York Herald Tribune*)

LEFT: King Leka, London, 1962. (Keystone) RIGHT: His Majesty King Leka, Madrid, 1972. (Gyenes)

LEFT: Their Imperial and Royal Highnesses Archduke Otto von Habsburg of Austria-Hungary and Archduchess Regina at the time of their wedding. Nancy, France, 1951. (Gyenes) RIGHT: Archduke Otto von Habsburg, London, 1963.

AUSTRIA-HUNGARY

Otto at home in Pocking, Bavaria, 1972. (Finlay)

Otto von Habsburg in discussion with students. Munich, 1973. (Finlay)

LEFT: Otto with three of his seven children: Princes Charles and George and Princess Monica. Pocking, Bavaria, 1972. (Finlay) RIGHT: Dr. Habsburg, Archduke Otto von Habsburg, or Emperor Otto I of Austria and King Otto II of Hungary. Pocking, 1972. (Finlay)

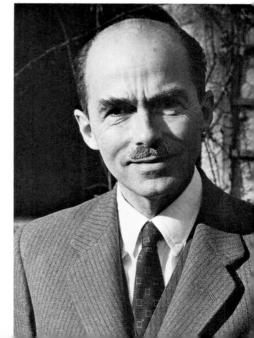

LEFT: Cadet S. Rylski, alias King Simeon of Bulgaria, Valley Forge, Pennsylvania, 1958. (Hartmann) RIGHT: The Bulgarian Royal Family: Princes Kardam, Kubrat, Konstantin Assen, and Kyril. Madrid, 1968.

BULGARIA

Crown Prince (now King) Simeon, age 6, with Bulgarian soldiers. 1942.

ABOVE: King Simeon and Queen Margarita, London, 1969. (Gyenes)

RIGHT: His Majesty King Simeon of Bulgaria. Madrid, 1966. (Talbot)

BELOW: King Simeon and Eastern Orthodox Bishop. New York, 1965. (Teliatnikow)

LEFT: Robert, Duke of Orleans, a former claimant, jailed for entering France. Paris, c. 1863. (Culver) RIGHT: A predecessor of Henri: Phillipe Count of Paris. c. 1890. (Culver)

FRANCE (BOURBON)

LEFT: The Count of Paris at General DeGaulle's funeral. RIGHT: Left to right: Duchess Irene of Greece, The Duke of Aosta, The Duchess of Aosta (Princess Claudia of France, daughter of The Count of Paris), baby Princess Bianca Irene of Aosta, The Count and Countess of Paris. 1966. (Both Keystone)

LEFT: At the death of the Bonaparte claimant's father, Prince Victor. Left to right: The Count of Flanders; his brother the Duke of Brabant (the future King Leopold of Belgium); Prince Louis Napoleon (the current claimant); King Albert of Belgium; Prince Louis, Victor's brother. Paris, 1926. (Culver) RIGHT: Prince Louis in his office—backed by his great-granduncle, Emperor Napoleon I, Paris, 1970. (Perrin)

FRANCE (BONAPARTE)

LEFT: Prince Louis, Princess Alix, and their children: Twins Princess Catherine and Prince Charles; Prince Jerome and Princess Laure. Pragins, 1962. (Perrin) RIGHT: Prince Charles, the Bonaparte Heir Apparent. 1970. (Perrin)

THE KINGDOM OF ALBANIA

His Majesty King Leka I
HOUSE OF ZOGOU

Albania comes first alphabetically; its royal house of Zogou comes last. The Albanian claimant also brings up the rear in the pecking order of dynastic antiquity. If, hypothetically, an ambitious royalty-watching hostess found herself in the velvet trap of having all the representatives of European royal houses for dinner, and did not know who took precedence over whom, she could fall back on the ploy of putting the oldest house nearest the salt. On this basis, His Majesty King Leka I would be very close to the pantry, since the kingdom of Albania was officially proclaimed only in 1928. From a nondynastic standpoint, this would be the hostess's loss: King Leka is young, attractive, and a bachelor.

Between World Wars I and II the tiny (eleven thousand square miles) kingdom of Albania was repeatedly in the news—primarily because of the volatility of Balkan politics, the tensions between Italy and Albania, and the personality of Leka's father, King Zog I. Albania's first sovereign had a reputation as a prime architect of Albanian independence from Turkey, a wardrobe of exotic uniforms, a beautiful queen with American connections, and a uniquely stylish manner. Zog was very much in evidence at the fashionable spas and conference tables of Europe in the early

1930s. On the eve of World War II, he lost his seat on the Albanian throne, but never relinquished the claim to it.

King Zog died in France in 1961 at the age of sixty-six without ever seeing his country again. He and the lovely Queen Geraldine, who was the former half-American Countess Apponyi de Nagy-Appony of Hungary, were forced to flee their country three days after the birth of their only son in Tirana, Albania, on April 4, 1939, when the Italians occupied the country. For political reasons the English refused to agree to the return of Zog to Albania after World War II. Albania was proclaimed a republic by the Communists in 1946, but Zog never abdicated. King Zog, a dapper, sleepy-eyed gentleman with a highly waxed moustache, lived with his family in England during the war, and in a small castle near Alexandria, Egypt, after the war. The king owned, but never lived in, a large estate on Long Island, New York, reputed to have been bought for a bucket of jewels. Upon Zog's death, according to the royal Constitution, Prince Leka succeeded him as the king of the Albanians. The coronation took place at the Bristol Hotel in Paris in the presence of a temporary National Assembly consisting of delegates and Albanian exiled monarchist dignitaries from all over the world.

King Leka is a tall, sturdy man of thirty-four years [1] who lives, unmarried, in Madrid, as does his mother, Queen Geraldine. Leka's office is at 194 Bravo Murillo. The general impression over the years is that the late King Zog was able to leave the country with a sizable personal fortune, and that most of it is still intact. Much of the remaining wealth is reputedly in gold. Neither Queen Geraldine nor her son has ever given any indication of impoverished circumstances; nor have they lived lavishly.

The king travels a great deal, principally with the purpose of visiting exiled Albanian communities in the Middle East, North and South America, and Southeast Asia. These communities, like

Leka himself, are predominantly Moslem, although there are also substantial numbers of Albanian Roman Catholic and Eastern Orthodox communities.

In July 1972 meetings were held in Madrid by the representatives of different Albanian political groups and organizations in exile. The king said that the "meetings were a great success as it is the first time in over twenty-three years that these parties and organizations have come together to discuss their political and ideological differences—with the result that a united front has been formed to fight against the oppression in Albania today."

Albanians living abroad claim that there remains in their country a relatively strong feeling for the monarchy,[2] and that that feeling, coupled with the dour way of life imposed by the current Communist regime, could react favorably toward any ambitions that King Leka might have. Leka is not passive on this subject. Indeed, when the British government first made rapprochement moves with the Chinese Communists, he complained "officially" about any diplomatic moves that would further sanction the alliance between the Red Chinese and the Albanian Communist government.

In November 1972 Albanian Moslems opened their first mosque in the New York area—in the Flatbush section of Brooklyn. Imam Isa Hoxha, the religious leader of the Albanian-American Islamic Center, said: "The reason for building our mosque is to bring the Albanian people together and to show Enver Hoxha [the present head of Albania] that the people still desire to keep their religion and their freedom alive." In 1967 all religious institutions were closed by the Communists, and Albania was declared "The World's first Atheistic State." New York has twenty thousand Albanians out of eighty thousand in the United States.

Though some Albanians migrated to the United States during the Balkan wars before 1914, the majority began to arrive after the

Communists took over in 1945. Most of the more recent arrivals were admitted under the liberalized immigration quotas of President John F. Kennedy's administration.

There are two million people in Albania. Perhaps there are many among them who hold onto the monarchial traditions. Albanians are tough, deeply religious people. They had to be to survive as people through five hundred years of Ottoman domination and three decades of Communist rule. There are several hundred thousands who live in exile. If memories are not too dim in the Albanian villages, and if free elections or a referendum could be held, King Leka could be an interesting candidate for the top job in the country he has not seen since he was three days old.

NOTES

1. Throughout the book all ages in years are as of mid-1973.

2. There is another, faint claim to the Albanian throne in the form of the heir of His Royal Highness Prince Wilhelm Frederick Henry of Wied, who was born in 1876, the second son of His Royal Highness Prince Wilhelm V. of Wied and Her Royal Highness Princess Marne of the Netherlands. Prince Wilhelm belonged to the sovereign House of Wied of the Holy Roman Empire, was a nephew of the Queen of Rumania, and also closely related to the royal houses of Greece, Austria, and Yugoslavia. Wilhelm was offered the throne by Germany and the other Great Powers in February 1914. He accepted it, became Monarch of Albania, and was ousted by September of the same year. He was nominated as a candidate for the throne of Lithuania by Germany, but the defeat of the Central Powers in World War I killed his chances. The last echo from Prince Wilhelm was in 1928 when he issued a statement of the claim when King Zog assumed the crown. It is not certain whether the son who survived him, His Royal Highness Prince Carol Victor, crown prince of Albania, or his next nearest heir, His Royal Highness Friedrick Wilhelm 8th Furst von Wied, is the pretender. Although Wilhelm was the first king of Albania, only eight months in the position and the passage of fifty-eight years make the Wied claim a mere whimper.

THE EMPIRE OF AUSTRIA
AND THE KINGDOM OF HUNGARY

His Imperial and Royal Highness Archduke Otto of Austria and King of Hungary
HOUSE OF HABSBURG-LORRAINE

There are substantial numbers of royalty-watchers who consider the House of Habsburg-Lorraine the absolute varsity. The Austro-Hungarian Empire is still a vibrant memory in the minds of many people living today, and the name of "Habsburg" continues to conjure up visions of power, legitimacy, and regal panoply. Along with Bourbon, Hohenzollern, and Windsor, the sound of the Habsburg name strikes a chord in the most untutored royalty buff. The custodian of the sovereign claim to the crowns of Austria and Hungary lives up to all expectations; His Imperial and Royal Highness Archduke Otto of Austria and Hungary—who prefers to be addressed as Dr. Habsburg—is an impressive and extraordinarily nice man.

Otto von Habsburg lives with his family in a small Bavarian town called Pocking, about twenty-five minutes by train from Munich. The town, hardly more than a village, lies in the rolling country which surrounds Lake Starnberg, the glittering sheet of strikingly clear water that has been Munich's watering place for generations. King Ludwig of Bavaria drowned here—the mad Ludwig struggling with his doctor and both men going down together is a difficult scene to imagine in such a serene setting.

The home of the Austro-Hungarian claimant is a rambling villa on the top of a hill, old and large, and with a faint air of benevolent decay, the balconies and stonework crumbling slightly. Inside there is an immediate impression of family life—lots of coats hanging in the hall, children appearing and disappearing, someone playing a violin badly upstairs, a large Alsatian dog whose ebullience has to be restrained when visitors arrive.

Otto, who is in his early sixties, has an irrepressible stamp of youth on his face and in the movements of his lean body. He exudes a sense of tremendous energy. After a meeting with Dr. Habsburg in the spring of 1972, my friend Ian Finlay of Dublin told me of his impressions:

". . . He is someone I couldn't imagine ever sitting still for ten minutes and doing nothing at all. He came bounding into the room [at the villa in Pocking], full of greetings in perfect English with an accent distinctly Austrian rather than German. He was keen to start [the interview] straight away, and chose to be interviewed in English, although I offered him German. He talked with great clarity and conviction, and frequently used my questions as the starting point for general disquisitions on subjects obviously central to his thinking. He has the ease and command of someone who does a great deal of public speaking. His intelligence and understanding of politics and international affairs are impressive. It is perhaps the mark of a true aristocrat that he was least happy talking about himself as an individual and about his family, and tended to steer such questions into broader ones.

"After the interview, which ended quite decisively, Otto courteously complimented me on my research; his impeccable courtesy was something that I shall never forget. When I had taken some photographs of him I said I would like to take one with some of his family. He disappeared and returned with a daughter, Monica, [sixteen], and two sons, Charles, [twelve], and George, [seven]. Monica's twin, Michaele, however, was missing. Later, when I was leaving, I met her in the hall and asked her why she didn't come and be in the photograph. She replied, 'Oh, Daddy said I couldn't be because I was wearing jeans and make-up.' Michaele, incidentally, is rather superlooking! As I was leaving, Otto was already launched into an intense conversation in fluent Hungarian with a theater director. . . ."

Archduke Otto was born near Reicheman, Austria, in 1912, the eldest child of Emperor Charles I of Austria (King Charles IV of Hungary) and of the empress and queen who was born Princess Zita of Bourbon-Parma. The Austrian National Assembly banished all Habsburgs from Austria in 1919 and confiscated the vast family properties. Any Habsburg who renounced all rights other than those of private citizens was allowed to live unmolested in Austria. The exiled King-Emperor Charles, however, renounced nothing; he returned to Hungary in 1921 to assert his claim to that throne. The Hungarian Parliament on November 21 forever abrogated the sovereign rights of Charles, and he died broken-hearted a year later.

The legitimists of Austria and Hungary, nevertheless, continued to consider Otto the rightful king-emperor since his father's death. Before the Anschluss in Austria on the eve of World War II, the Workers' party, known as the Christian Syndicates, called unsuccessfully for Otto's return.

In an interview given to a French newspaperwoman in 1950, Archduke Otto stated that Hitler offered him the opportunity to return to the Habsburg throne if he accepted and supported the Nazi ideology. He also stated that the Russians, in the late 1940s, intimated that an agreement with them was not out of the question. Otto refused both.

In March 1951, Otto married Princess Regina of Saxe-Meiningen, in Nancy, France. Regina, forty-seven, is the daughter of Prince George of Saxe-Meiningen and Princess Clara Maria, the former Countess von Korff. During the war Otto lived in Washington, D. C., and since then he and his family have lived at various times in Luxembourg, England, and Germany. Emperor Otto I of Austria and King Otto II of Hungary, as he is considered by the legitimists, has five daughters and two sons by Regina, ranging in age from nineteen to eight years.

After World War II Archduke Otto returned to Austria but was later banished from the country by the Soviets, who were the occupying power. He and the family were permitted to reenter Austria by order of the Austrian Supreme Court in 1966.

Otto von Habsburg is extremely active in the world of political science—particularly as it relates to the European unification. His views of the world situation, and his dedication to the solution to the problems therein, are logical and appealing. (*See* Interview, p. 119.) Otto writes a regular newspaper column on world affairs, which is published simultaneously in Austria, Spain, Portugal, France, Belgium, Germany, Brazil, Peru, and in a number of papers in North America. Otto has traveled widely, and is in constant demand as a lecturer in universities and other academic circles in many countries. He has written twelve books on political science, world affairs, and history.

Otto is a man of many worthy parts, a most interesting and friendly person. He would make a first-rate professor, diplomat, president, or friend. He has a certain political charisma that, in the United States, coupled with some familiarity with commercial matters, woud make him a superior candidate for political office.

In June 1972 it was announced that Otto and his family would return to Austria. *The New York Times* (June 3) reported that "Dr. Habsburg and his family will leave exile in Bavaria, and return to Austria to live." It also stated that the claimant's mother, "80 year old Empress Zita, who lives in Switzerland, disapproves." These moves provoke conjecture.

There is certainly some royalist sympathy ingrained in parts of the Austrian and Hungarian spirits, but Dr. Habsburg avoids capitalizing on it or even discussing it in specific relation to the Habsburgs. If monarchist sentiments were permitted to flourish, and did, there is no question that Archduke Otto would offer a uniquely attractive prospect for leadership. Otto von Habsburg is a man for all seasons. Perhaps a season approaches.

THE KINGDOM OF BULGARIA

His Majesty King Simeon II
HOUSE OF SAXE-COBURG AND GOTHA

In mid-1972 Queen Elizabeth of England made a visit to Sofia. This occasion was not calculated to elate the morale of her cousin, King Simeon II of the Bulgarians, who waits and works in Spain for the opportunity to repossess the crown of Bulgaria, and to hasten the expulsion of the Marxist regime.

The House of Saxe-Coburg and Gotha, one of the oldest Germanic dynasties, spawned the royal houses of Bulgaria, Great Britain, Belgium, and Portugal. In its days of power, blood was demonstrably thicker than water; today one member of the family officially recognizes the alien regime that ousted the other member—presumably on the theory that political expediency is thicker than blood. There is no bitterness between Simeon and his British cousin: both understand—and sympathize—with the other's position. This sophistication, however, does not blunt the Bulgarian claimant's faith and hope.

King Simeon II was born in Sofia in 1937, the second child and only son of King Boris and Queen Giovanna, princess of Savoy, daughter of King Victor Emmanuel of Italy and sister of King Umberto, the Italian claimant. Simeon was only six years old when his father died, and a Council of Regents was appointed to admin-

ister the government pending his majority. Simeon's uncle, Prince
Kyril, a coregent, was executed by the Communists in 1945 with
225 other former ministers and members of Parliament. The king
went into exile in Egypt in September 1946 with his mother and
his sister, Princess Marie Louise, when the Communists instituted
the Bulgarian Republic after a hastily called referendum. In 1950
the Egyptian police arrested two Bulgarian Communists who arrived by ship in Alexandria, reputedly on a mission to assassinate
King Simeon.

In January 1962 in Vevy, Switzerland, King Simeon married
dona Margarita Gomez-Acebo y Cejuela, the daughter of a Spanish marquis who was executed, with his wife, by the Spanish Loyal-
ists near Madrid in 1936. Simeon and thirty-seven-year-old Queen
Margarita have four sons: Prince Kardam, ten, heir to the throne,
Prince Kyril, eight, Prince Kubat, seven, and Prince Konstantin
Assen, five—and a daughter, Princess Kalina, one. Queen Margarita is directly related, by marriage, to the Spanish royal family.

King Simeon went to primary school in Bulgaria, Victoria College in Alexandria, Egypt, The Lycée Français de Madrid, and
the Valley Forge Military Academy in Wayne, Pennsylvania (under the name of Mr. Eylski, Cadet #6883), where he graduated in
1959. He has also studied law and political science under private
tutors.

King Simeon is tall, slim, and fair. He wears a trim beard. He
speaks Bulgarian, Spanish, English, and French. Margarita is slight
and dark, and is exceedingly friendly and intelligent.

Simeon and Margarita live in Madrid and in Crans-sur-Sierre,
Switzerland, with their five children. Simeon describes his occupation as a "jack-of-all-trades, primarily interested in business, banking, and politics—some call it 'statesmanship.' " His hobbies are
anthropology, reading, aviation, and politics. Simeon is reasonably

comfortable financially—providing, as he says, that he can go on working as hard as he does.

There is probably no sovereign in exile who works more actively: his numerous business activities in banking and investments help him to support his political efforts. The king spends a great deal of time in correspondence with Bulgarians who seek jobs, financial help, family assistance. His chancellory, under Colonel George I. Guentcheff, head of His Majesty's office at 3 Avenida del Valle in Madrid, publishes a monthly bulletin which is sent to Bulgarians living abroad and to friends and supporters. There are some hundred and fifty thousand people of Bulgarian origin scattered outside their country, principally in the Argentine, Australia, Canada, France, Germany, Israel, and the United States.

King Simeon is totally serious and active in his cause to regain the Bulgarian throne. He has stated that he is constitutionally in the twenty-ninth year of his reign, since he never abdicated. He believes that the resentments that have grown among his people, and the irrepressible evolution of Communist regimes, will eventually force the end of the present system and permit a return of the monarchy. He works incessantly within the framework of this thought.

In 1972 Simeon said: ". . . A monarchial form of government would be particularly timely now after years of heavy-handed dictatorship. It would, of course, be pointless to pretend that there are not times when a King finds the burdens of his task heavy and discouraging. In the numerous times of difficulty, lack of support, attacks without grounds against the dynasty, and the humiliations of the life of an exile, I must admit that doubts and even despair arise in my mind." But Simeon is a strong fighter, and a patient one. He recognizes the bitterness that the exiles and the suppressed sympathizers in Bulgaria may feel. In 1969 Simeon made a declaration that ended with this sentiment: ". . . The desire for revenge and the feeling of hatred must be overcome to achieve true national reconciliation and unity. With the support of all the Bulgarian people—for right is on our side—we shall create together a just and modern government. We Bulgarians look confidently to the future convinced that freedom, justice, and welfare will finally triumph in our land. This is the ultimate goal in life of him who is still King of the Bulgarians and whose thoughts are constantly turned towards Bulgaria."

The Communist regime in Bulgaria recently celebrated the twenty-fifth anniversary of the "popular republic." Simeon challenges that popularity, and seeks the occasion to prove it. He might possibly find it. The only certainty in Balkan politics is their unpredictability. On the counts of decency, intelligence, and fairmindedness, no constituency could ask for a more attractive spokesman. As a Bulgarian elevator operator in Pittsburgh commented in 1971: "Simeon's father was a wonderful fellow. Why doesn't his son have a chance to do something for the old country? Why should he sit in Spain? He belongs in Sofia."

THE KINGDOM OF FRANCE
AND THE FRENCH EMPIRE

There are two valid claimants to the French throne. Each is an able man, and each has his coterie of supporters. One is the chief of the house of France, the family of Bourbon-Orléans; the other is recognized head of the French Bonapartists.

1) His Royal Highness, Monseigneur Henri d'Orléans, Count of Paris

HOUSE OF CAPET: ORLÉANS BRANCH

There is something stunningly special about the royal house of France and the current claim to its throne: a certain elegance of style, an unshakable belief in its cause, and, at least publicly, a family solidarity that broaches no trespass or tarnishment. Longevity and centuries of power have molded a unique quality into the character of the French royal family. This may be due, in large measure, to the impressive fact that the royal house of France ruled for almost nine hundred years, with relatively brief interruptions by the French Revolution and the empire of the Bonapartes. This is quite long enough for a royal line to develop distinct survival mores, and a sense of its own importance.

Hugh Capet became king of France in 987, and his male descendants followed him to the throne without interruption for about four hundred years. Cousinly branches then took over the crown in succeeding generations until 1848 when the last monarch, King Louis-Philippe, was overthrown.

From the viewpoint of Monseigneur Henri d'Orléans, Count of Paris, the current claimant to the French crown, the monarchy has been gone for only 125 years, and that amount of time can perhaps eventually be considered as another fairly brief interruption. Henri and his family have always conducted themselves in an impeccable fashion: *royauté oblige.* Suitable marriages are arranged, scandal and frivolous involvements are not tolerated, and a destiny-imposed dedication to France is the rule of the house.

The Count of Paris behaves as though he were Henri VI, king of France—which, *de jure,* in the eyes of the monarchists, he is. This does not mean that he flaunts his position, is condescending in his manner, autocratic, or aggressive. He gives the clear impression, however, that he is indeed the custodian of an ancient and currently valid claim and, to a certain number of his countrymen, the Keeper of the Flame. The French governments since the fall of the monarchy seemed to recognize the latent appeal and unquestioned legitimacy of the royal house, and cautiously allowed the Count of Paris and his family to return to France only twenty-odd years ago. In the order of antiquity, the French crown is the oldest: at a table with his peers, Henri would most certainly be nearest the salt—and he would have it no other way.[1]

Monseigneur Henri of Orléans, the Count of Paris, was born in the Chateau of Nouvion-en-Thierache in Aisne, France, on July 5, 1908. He is the only son and fourth child of the Duke de Guise, Jean III, and the former Princess Isabelle of Orléans. Henri spent his childhood in French Morocco, near Larache, where his parents went to live in 1909. After World War I, Henri studied at the Catholic University of Angers. When his uncle, the head of the house, died in 1926, he went into exile with his father, the claimant, and the others of his immediate family.

The royal family moved near Brussels, and Henri went to the University of Louvain. After his marriage, the present Count and Countess of Paris lived in the Chateau d'Agimont near the Belgian-French border. The Count owned and edited two newspapers in Belgium for circulation in France during his exile—*Le Courier Royal* and *Ici France.*

In 1939 the Count of Paris was refused permission by the governments of France and England to serve in their armies—strictly because of the political implications of Henri's royal status. He eventually served in the French Foreign Legion for one year. After World War II the family lived in Pamplona, Spain, and in Sintra, Portugal.

The Count of Paris was married in Sicily forty-two years ago to Her Imperial and Royal Highness Princess Isabelle d'Orléans et Braganza, a cousin, who was the daughter of His Royal Highness Prince Pierre d'Orléans et Braganza and Countess Dobrzensky. Henri and Isabelle have reared a robust brood of eleven royal offspring—four sons and seven daughters ranging in age from forty to twenty-four years. The married daughters have as husbands an Austrian count, a Belgian count, a royal Spanish prince, a royal German duke, a royal Italian prince, and a French baron; three of the sons have married a royal German princess, a French countess, and a French duke's daughter; one son is deceased, and one is unmarried.[2]

In 1950 the French Parliament abrogated the 1886 Law of Exile, thereby permitting the Count of Paris and his family to return to France. They live in the Manor of Coeur-Volant in Louveciennes near Paris. Since his return to his homeland, Henri has become involved in French political life, principally through the publication by his office of his *Monthly Information Bulletin from the*

Political Office of Monseigneur the Count of Paris (120 bis, rue de Miromesnil, Paris) in which he comments on current political, economic, and social problems. It has a circulation of twenty thousand.

The Count of Paris speaks French, English, Spanish, German, and Italian—all with fluency and style. He is a slight, neat man with sleek hair, blue eyes, and a moustache. The count is reserved and cautious. He takes his position most seriously, is a warm pater-familias, and a good if careful public speaker.

After politics, agriculture (in which he is an expert) is Henri's favorite occupation. He is also an amateur pilot and an excellent horseman. The count's extremely democratic ideas have at times surprised the traditional monarchists. He is most popular with the core of the Monarchist party who view him as the solution to France's chronic political ills. Many historians and political analysts feel that Charles de Gaulle was definitely a traditionalist and possibly a royalist at heart. If the imagination of the French voters could have been stirred, or if it had seemed to be politically expedient to lend some quiet support to the monarchist movement in France, General de Gaulle would have done it. It is still possible. The French have a logical and realistic turn of mind. They are also the masters of controlled pomp and the respecters of special circumstances. The Count of Paris has indisputable qualities that could be assets, in some way, to France and to her dignity. He might be summoned to an appointive position. With some luck and effort, and a higher profile on the part of the French royalists, it is conceivable that the present "brief interruption" in the monarchy could be brought to a close.

2)   His Imperial Highness, Prince Louis Napoleon Bonaparte
HOUSE OF BONAPARTE

One of the enduring success stories of all time is that of the Bonaparte family. From obscure beginnings in Genoa and minor functionary positions in Corsica, this feisty, resilient, and well-organized family eventually held sway over most of Europe and established an imperial dynasty that influenced history for all time. In the business of kingship, Napoleon Bonaparte was the archetypical chairman of the board and chief executive officer.

Napoleon I started in the "company" at the bottom rung, was promoted to management (General), then to senior vice-president (First Consul), and soon after to chairman (Emperor). He then consolidated his position by becoming the principal stockholder as well: he married a large shareholder, (Archduchess Marie Louise of Austria), and set the stage for a series of spectacular take-overs. The Bonaparte family moved into prime control of the business of European sovereignty. The entire saga took less than a hundred years.

Emperor Napoleon I had five brothers. The youngest, Jerome, was king of Westphalia, and is the great-grandfather of the present claimant to the French imperial throne, His Imperial Highness Louis-Jerome-Victor-Emmanuel-Leopold-Marie, Prince Napoleon Bonaparte. If Napoleon I had been the type to retire quietly after hand-picking his successor to the chairmanship, he could have done so with pride and confidence in the person of the current claimant.

Prince Napoleon Bonaparte was born in Brussels fifty-eight years ago, the only son of Prince Victor and Princess Clementine of Belgium, duchess of Saxony. Louis grew up in Belgium; his father died when Louis was only twelve years old. As a very young child he also lived in Farnborough, England, with his family, who fled Belgium during the German invasion of World War I. The Prince was privately tutored and also attended the Universities of Louvain in Belgium and Lausanne in Switzerland.

Although the Law of Exile excluded both claimants to the French throne from France until 1950, Prince Louis was permitted to live in Paris, under the name of Monsieur de Montfort, in appreciation of the services which he rendered to France during World War II, as an officer in the Resistance—principally under General Koenig—and for which he was awarded the Legion of Honor and the Croix de Guerre. Before joining Koenig's forces, Louis also served in the French Foreign Legion under a false name.

In 1949 Prince Louis was married to Alix de Foresta, who was born in Marseilles in 1926, the daughter of Count and Countess Alberic de Foresta, a very old family of Italian origin. The prince requested permission to hold the wedding in the Chapelle des Invalides, the Tomb of Napoleon I, but was refused by the government, and they were married in the small village of Liniéres-Bouton in Maine-et-Loire. (The prince's niece, Countess Isabella de Witt, daughter of Her Imperial Highness Princess Marie Clothilde Bonaparte and Count Serge de Witt, was, however, married in the Chapelle des Invalides in October 1971 to Monsieur Remmart.)

Prince Louis and Princess Alix have two sons, Prince Charles, twenty-one, and Prince Jerome, fifteen, and two daughters, Princess Catherine, Charles's twin, and Princess Laure, twenty. The imperial family lives in a comfortable, informal villa in Pragins and on the Boulevard Suchet in Paris.

An untutored view of His Imperial Highness Prince Louis, Napoleon Bonaparte, vis-à-vis His Royal Highness Monseigneur Henri d'Orléans, the Count of Paris, might tend to characterize

Louis's claim as "lesser" than Henri's. This would not be quite accurate. It is more of a question of the *ancien régime* versus the empire: the royal house versus the imperial house. From the standpoint of validity, both claimants are equal; from the standpoint of legitimate antiquity, however, the royal house remains unique.

It would not be correct for the casual royalty-watcher to dismiss the Bonapartist claim as that stemming from an upstart or usurper. While Napoleon I did create the office of "emperor" and put himself in it, he and his heirs were wise and successful enough to marry into the ruling families of their times so that in many countries the Bonaparte or imperial family became intertwined with the *anciens régimes* of the times. This has resulted in the fact that today Prince Louis is connected with all the sovereign families of Europe—and is, indeed, descended several ways from King Louis XIV. Prince Louis is the great-grandnephew of Napoleon I, the great-grandson of King Jerome-Napoleon and of King Victor Emmanuel of Italy, and the grandson of King Leopold II of Belgium.

Prince Louis is a tall, powerful, athletic figure. He is a strong swimmer, skier, sailor, scuba diver, race driver, horseman, and pilot. Louis is an active and successful businessman, serving on the boards of several European manufacturing and marketing companies; he has worked on the economic and industrial development of the Congo, and has investments in coffee plantations, orange groves, and property in Chad and Corsica.

Prince Louis is widely traveled and speaks French, English, German, Italian, and Spanish. He is not in the front line of politics. While interested and well informed, he does not parade his claim. His secretariat (at 1 rue Ernest-Herbert in Paris) is a business office, not a political bureau. When asked about his position as claimant—or pretender—Prince Louis says that the present Napoleon Bonaparte (himself) is first and foremost a man of *this* epoque, the twentieth century; a man of both his own country and of

Europe. He says that, like any dedicated and willing citizen, he is "available" to his country. Louis feels that if, some day, a majority of his fellow citizens want him to assume some national responsibility, he would not be disobedient to their wishes. But he stresses firmly that he always forbids the use of his name or his person for partisan political purposes. The name of *Napoleon* is, in his eyes, a synonym of *union*.

The Bonapartist "party" in France keeps a very low profile. Strangely enough, however, there is a certain mystique to the Napoleonic name. Napoleon I had immense appeal for the average man. A large majority of the common people of his time saw Napoleon as a champion who could provide peace, and do away with the feudal injustices that had held so many Europeans in thrall for so many centuries. Some historians see Napoleon Bonaparte I as the first romantic nationalist or possibly the first architect of a united Europe.

France's foreign territories have shrunk throughout the world. The *empire* does not exist; therefore, by deduction, France's *imperial house* is an anachronism. *"Vive l'empereur!"* would have no meaning. But Prince Louis Napoleon Bonaparte is not an anachronism, and any resurgence of monarchist feeling in France would probably take this into consideration. France has, in the past, returned to a king after a republic. The chances are very slight for Prince Louis—but *not* nonexistent like his great-grandfather's empire.

NOTES

1. An ironic twist of history has created another pretender to the French monarchy, rivaling in a most tenuous fashion the claims of Henri, Count of Paris: The third pretender is Henri de Bourbon, duke de Bourgoyne who, though not exiled, lived after World War II in Casablanca as a salesman for agricultural machinery. His current whereabouts are unknown.

This Henri de Bourbon is claimed by some to be the direct descendant of Louis XVII, who was imprisoned as a child during the 1789 revolution and scheduled for the guillotine. Official French history records that young Prince Louis died in prison. Others believe that a changeling was substituted, and that the royal prince was carried off to Prussia, where he lived for many years under the name of Naundorff, and returned to France in 1833 to press, in vain, his claim to the throne during the reign of King Louis-Philippe.

It is pathetic to note that at the time of Naundorff's presence in France, Louis XVII's surviving sister, Madame Royale, Duchess d'Angoulême, might have settled the dispute, but obstinately refused to see him, probably for political reasons relative to the recently reestablished French monarchy. In 1852 she did, however, make a will in which she is supposed to have given the true facts with the stipulation that it not be opened before the passing of a hundred and fifty years. The document was sealed and placed in the vaults of the Vatican. This may offer a challenge to royalty-watchers having good connections with the Holy See.

My friend, author-attorney Louis Auchincloss of New York, brought to my attention in 1972 still another pretender to the Bourbon crown, who has the distinctly un-Gallic name of Henri Freeman. Auchincloss wrote to me as follows: "When the Duc de Berry was in exile in Britain during the era of the First Empire with his father, the Comte d'Artois, he formed a liaison with an English woman called Amy Brown. By Amy Brown he had two daughters, presumably illegitimate, who were later given titles on Berry's deathbed by his uncle, Louis XVIII. One was Comtesse d'Issoudun and the other's name escapes me.

"After the Resoration, Amy Brown moved to Paris and lived there to be a very old woman, dying as late as 1876. She lived in modest retirement in the Faubourg St. Germain and was called upon by members of the Royal Family and treated with great respect by the 'gratin' [upper crust].

"However, she brought with her to Paris four children (older half-brothers and half-sister of the above mentioned two ladies) who were commonly supposed to have been her children by other men and born prior to her liaison with Berry. These four children were John Freeman (born 1801), Robert Freeman (born 1803), Emma Marshall (born 1804) and George Brown (born 1805). The descendants of the oldest of these, John Freeman, maintained that Amy Brown had been legally married to Berry prior to 1801 and that not only the two ladies ennobled by Louis XVIII but all four of the Freeman-Marshall-Brown brood were legitimate children of Berry and Amy Brown.

"If this claim is true, obviously the primary male line of Amy's oldest child, John Freeman, are the *rightful* inheritors of the French throne and always were, going even before the Comte de Chambord. Indeed, their claim would render the Comte de Chambord a bastard son of Berry. The present

Freeman pretender, Henri, was born in 1929. He was married to and divorced by a New York girl called Jacqueline DeVoe who resumed her maiden name after the divorce and I believe continues to live in Manhattan although she was listed in last year's Social Register, but not this year's.

"The thing that makes me suspect there might be something in the Freeman claim is that they were able to marry so well. Of course, the bastards of royalty notoriously can marry into the nobility, or even other royalties, but these Freemans, if their claim is wrong, were not even the bastards of Berry, but of Amy's former lovers!"

2. Princess Isabelle, 40, is married to His Royal Highness Count Frederick-Charles de Sobonborn-Buchheim, 34; Prince Henri, 39, to Her Royal Highness Duchesse Maria-Theresa de Württemberg, 38; Princess Helene-Astrid, 38, to Count Evrard de Limburg-Stirum, 45; Prince François was killed at the age of 37 in the Algerian war in 1960; Princess Anne, 34, is married to His Royal Highness Prince Carlos of Bourbon-Two Sicilies, 34; Princess Diane, 32, to His Royal Highness Duke Carlo de Württemberg, 36, (Maria-Theresa's brother); Prince Michael, 31, to Pasquier de Franclieu, 31; Prince Jacques (Michael's twin) to Gersende de Sabran-Ponteves, 30, daughter of the Duke de Sabran; Princess Claude, 29, to Prince Amedeo di Savoia; Princess Chantal, 26, to Baron François-Xavier de Sambucy de Sorgue, 27; Prince Thibaud, 24, is unmarried. Prince Michael's marriage in 1967 did not receive the official sanction by the Count of Paris as head of the royal house of France; the dynastic rights of Prince Michael and his children were, therefore, forfeited.

THE EMPIRE OF GERMANY
AND THE KINGDOM OF PRUSSIA

His Imperial and Royal Highness Prince Louis-Ferdinand
HOUSE OF HOHENZOLLERN

The year 1971 marked the one hundredth anniversary of the German Empire which Kaiser Wilhelm I created when he federated the various German principalities under his rule. Prior to that the powerful Hohenzollern family had been flexing its muscles since the tenth century. They were feudal nobles, then counts, princes, dukes, and, by 1700, kings of Prussia. In 1871 they also became emperors of Germany. The last king-emperor was Kaiser Wilhelm II, who lost his crown after the German defeat in World War I. The current claimant to the empire of Germany and the kingdom of Prussia is His Imperial and Royal Highness Prince Louis-Ferdinand. There is little of the strutting imperialist in this heir to the Hohenzollern leadership, which reaches back into history for almost a thousand years.

Prince Louis-Ferdinand's Berlin home is a white modern bungalow in the suburbs, which he had built a few years ago. The house carries the rather trite name of "Mon Bijou." The interior is furnished in modern German taste and seems somehow empty and unlived in—quite unlike the claimant himself, who is immensely friendly and easygoing. Louis-Ferdinand speaks English fluently in an accent that clearly reflects his stay in America many years ago.

Prince Louis-Ferdinand cares about his claim and his position, and keeps acutely informed on all political matters. But his life, at the moment, seems a trifle unambitious with regard to these matters. He is an overt admirer, on the other hand, of Otto von Habsburg and his activities.

Ian Finlay told me of his lunch with Louis-Ferdinand in March 1972:

". . . We had superb food served by a discreet and elderly butler on a table lit by four white candles. I was encouraged to sample three different white wines, and the meal ended with the best lemon soufflé I have ever eaten. When I left, Louis presented me with a signed copy of his autobiography, and an invitation to join him at a musical soiree at Hohenzollern Castle in July. Louis struck me as being a very open, hospitable man but rather naïve. Perhaps typical of his approach is his notion that if only his grandfather, the Kaiser, had gone to America, there would have been no war because he and the Americans would have liked each other so much! . . . ."

Prince Louis-Ferdinand was born sixty-six years ago in the Chateau of Marmon near Potsdam. He is the second son of Crown Prince Frederick Wilhelm, imperial German prince and royal prince of Prussia, and the former Cecily, duchess of Mecklenburg. His father died in 1951 in his small house in Hechingen, which was in the French zone of occupied Germany. Frederick Wilhelm was the eldest son of the Kaiser and grandson of Queen Victoria of England. Since World War II, in which all his properties were confiscated, the claimant's father lived frugally with one servant, and during the last years of his life, received many foreign visitors. He spoke English without an accent and had many of the characteristics of the British country gentleman. His favorite subject was how the monarchy could have helped Germany in the post-World War I years. As head of the imperial family, the late crown prince appeared in public for the last time at the marriage of his daughter, Princess Cecily, to an interior decorator, Clyde K. Harris of Texas, in the Hohenzollern castle at Sigmaringen. He, Frederick Wilhelm, heir to the crowns of Prussia and the German Empire, abdicated his dynastic rights in 1918. His eldest son, Wilhelm, became head of the family. In 1933, following Crown Prince Wilhelm's renunciation of his dynastic rights when he married a commoner, his brother, Louis-Ferdinand, became the heir of the House of Hohenzollern and chief of the imperial and royal house.

In 1938, in Potsdam, Louis-Ferdinand married the Grand Duchess Kyra Cyrilovna of Russia, who died in France in 1967. Kyra was the elder sister of Grand Duke Vladimir, the present claimant to the Russian throne, and the daughter of Grand Duke Cyril, head of the imperial Russian house, and Grand Duchess Victoria Feodorovna, who was the former princess of Saxe-Coburg and Gotha, princess of Great Britain and Northern Ireland, and duchess of Saxony.

Louis-Ferdinand and Kyra have four sons and three daughters. The two elder princes married commoners, and the third eldest child, Princess Marie-Cecile, married Duke Frederick-August of Oldenburg, son of His Royal Highness, the Hereditary Grand Duke of Oldenburg and his first wife, the former Princess Helen of Waldeck and Pyrmont.

Prince Louis-Ferdinand had a rather colorful fling in America before his marriage; he became a good friend of President Franklin Roosevelt, Henry Ford, Charlie Chaplin, Eddie Rickenbacker, and many other celebrities. His love affair with Lili Damita, the ex-Mrs. Errol Flynn, made excellent tabloid copy for months. He and Kyra visited the Roosevelts in 1937, and he returned again to the United States in connection with the publishing of his autobiography, *Rebel Prince.*

After World War II, Prince Louis-Ferdinand believed there was still a feeling of tenderness for the Hohenzollern dynasty in Germany. Although he did not, in any way, work toward a restoration of the monarchy, Louis-Ferdinand seemed to be quite popular among his own people in Germany, as well as with the Allied occupation authorities. His participation in the plot to overthrow Hitler during the war culminated a record of quiet resistance to the Nazi totalitarianism. Twenty years ago Louis-Ferdinand's younger brother, Prince Frederick ("Fritzi") George, publicly stated that a return of the monarchy was a remotely conceivable possibility in these days of political fantasies. In 1950 Prince "Fritzi" endorsed this faint hope by filing for the right to resume his full and legal title of Prince Frederick George Wilhelm Christof of Prussia. From 1945 Fritzi had lived in England as a farmer and a naturalized British subject under the name of George Mansfield. Said he: "It's only a question of establishing legally my correct family name and title. The name of Mansfield was merely a convenience in my business dealings on the farm."

One of the homes of the imperial family, Kronberg Castle, near Frankfurt, was in the custody of the United States occupation authority during the Second World War. In 1945 it was the scene of a sensational theft when a United States colonel and his wife entered the palace and made off with the Hessian crown jewels. In 1951 it was the scene of another act of American *lèse-majesté* when the United States occupation forces' high school in Frankfurt held its jitterbugging senior prom there. As a Hamburg-based American army major exclaimed to a *New York Herald Tribune* reporter that year: "I think the average German might be pleased —or something akin to it—if we would give some of these confiscated lands and property back to a few of the old, clean, noble families—like the Hohenzollerns. As a matter of fact, I don't think they'd mind a bit if we gave back the whole country to the Hohenzollerns. At least they would be a rallying point."

Louis-Ferdinand is an amiable, generous man. He is good-looking, pleasant in his style, and rather gentle in his ways. The crown prince lives in a large, family-oriented house in Bremen-Borgfeld, Germany, and also in a modern house on Koeningsalle (ironically, "King's Way") in the suburbs of Berlin.

Louis-Ferdinand is relatively well off financially. The Hohenzollerns had large properties in the present East Germany, which were confiscated. But the family has substantial investments—shares in West German companies as well as United States, British, and other European securities. The crown prince spends a large part of his time administering what remains of their holdings. He is also politically active in the sense that he is on good terms with all non-Communist activists, and makes his Berlin home a center for discussion of all aspects of German life. Louis-Ferdinand is outwardly a supporter of a united Europe. (*See* Interview, p. 137.)

The German claimant certainly must react to the unofficial polls, which indicate that as much as 30 percent of the present German population has monarchist sympathies. The definition of "sympathy" is the crucial point in this case. As Prince Louis-Ferdinand says, nothing is impossible in politics today. The Hohenzollerns did well by Germany; Germans psychically like a leader—with or without credentials. Prince Louis-Ferdinand represents a legitimate leadership. If current European politics became tumultuous and filled with *angst,* it is not at all frivolous to conceive that the traditionalists could recapture the imaginations of the Germans: The spotlight would immediately and correctly focus on Prince Louis-Ferdinand of Prussia.

A new "political center" was created in West Germany in December 1972 when Willy Brandt's government coalition won a parliamentary majority. *The New York Times* noted that "for the first time, whole states that had been fortresses of conservatism—Schleswig-Holstein and Lower Saxony in the north, the Rhineland Palatinate and the Saar in the southwest—went strongly for Mr. Brandt's Social Democrats and Foreign Minister Scheel's Free Democrats. . . . The coalition drew new strength from categories previously considered safe for the opposition Christian Union parties: farmers, older women, middle-rank business employees, and Catholics. . . ." These are traditionalist people who have, in the past, rallied strongly to the monarchist concept. A strong political center in West Germany, which harbors any sympathy for the good old days of the Hollenzollerns, could mean something to Louis-Ferdinand and his family.

Prince Louis-Ferdinand is in his mid-sixties. A time to "retire" perhaps. But a claimant cannot retire. His "business" will not let him. (G. Mennen Williams, when governor of Michigan, once asked Louis what his business was. When Louis told him that his basic business was that of claimant, the governor asked if it paid well. The Prince replied that he did not know—*yet*.) Louis's two eldest sons are excluded from the claimancy because of their marriages to commoners. But he has other sons, not married.

Louis-Ferdinand is ready and certainly willing to be called to his family's basic "business." He could do it well—not spectacularly but quietly, and with a certain amount of strangely bourgeois naïveté and schmaltz. He could set the stage for his successor—a modern, unaffected, well-informed young Hollenzollern.

There are a fair amount of people in Germany who would find this alternative not unattractive. The prospect is alive and well and living in Germany.

THE KINGDOM OF IRELAND

Ireland is a strange and unique territory for the postgraduate royalty-watcher. The invasions, occupations, struggles, battles, and wars that have swept across this island over the centuries have virtually obliterated the ancient, native, Gaelic royal dynasties— at least the expected evidences and trappings of them.[1] The Irish, from time immemorial, however, have been ardent genealogists bent on preserving the identities and relationships of their tribes, clans, septs, and families in the face of great opposition—particularly during the invasions and occupations by the Danes, the Normans, and the English.

For almost eight hundred years the English carried out the aim to subdue on their flank the alien Gaels whose language, customs, laws, legends, myths, culture, and eventually religion differed from Anglo-Saxon-Norman Britain. The English were ultimately successful in their similar objectives with the Scots, the Welsh, the Cornish, and others on the island of Britain. Today they are one nation. But Ireland survives as—or has become again—a nation unto itself. The Irish island is *almost* whole. There remains, of course, Northern Ireland, which is still a part of Great Britain; and the ancient animosities are still aflame there.

To subdue a nation, the first essential is to destroy or render impotent the nation's leadership: the kings, the chiefs, the spiritual and intellectual powers, the aristocracy. This was done very effectively by the English in Ireland. The old, royal, noble, and aristocratic native families were mostly killed, banished into exile, impoverished, or, in many cases, married into. This fact, over the centuries, has wiped off the face of the land the easily recognizable traces of the historical Gaelic supremacy. Today, a poor farmer living desperately in the wilds of Connemara may have valid and traceable direct bloodlines back to a High King of Ireland, and be infinitely more aristocratic, indeed, royal than the earl who lives splendidly in his castle, and whose family has thrived over the generations by the grace of the English supremacy in Ireland.

This makes it difficult for any but the most intrepid royalty-watcher to find what he seeks in Ireland. But it is worth the search. A seeker in Ireland must combine certain characteristics of the archaeologist, anthropologist, librarian, hiker, sportsman, and *bon vivant*. In Eire he needs a pair of Wellingtons, sturdy walking shoes, a black tie, a tolerance for strong spirits, a vague appreciation of the Celtic twilight, and a working knowledge of premedieval and medieval English, Scottish, Danish, French, and Spanish history.

The royalty-watcher in Ireland may find himself in a bog in Mayo, on a sheep farm in Roscommon, in a regency dining room in Limerick, or at a hunt ball in a castle in Meath. Anywhere.

There are three totally legitimate claimants—pretenders, if you will—to the Irish throne. All trace their royal lines back directly to the High Kingship. Two of the families became historically allied, by marriage and politics, with the English ascendancy; the other did not, and has survived startlingly intact in its old, native Irishness. Ironically, in these days of strife and violence in Ireland, one claimant is a Roman Catholic and the others are Protestants. Of further irony is the fact that, undoubtedly, they were interrelated many centuries ago. Within this time-encrusted fact may lie a clue to an ultimate solution to Ireland's heart-wrenching problems.

LEFT: Their Imperial and Royal Highnesses Prince Louis-Ferdinand and the late Princess Kyra of Prussia with their seven children. Berlin, 1966. RIGHT: Prince Louis-Ferdinand. Berlin, 1972. (Finlay)

GERMANY

BELOW RIGHT: Crown Prince Louis-Ferdinand and his fourth son, Prince Christian-Sigismond von Hohenzollern. Berlin, 1972. (Finlay)

ABOVE: The German claimant at home. Berlin, 1972. (Finlay)

LEFT: The O'Conor don, the Reverend Charles Davis Mary Joseph Anthony O'Conor, S. J. Naas, Co. Kildare, 1972. (Finlay)

BELOW: Miss Josephine O'Conor, sister of the claimant and Chatelaine of Clonalis. Co. Roscommon, 1972. (CARA)

IRELAND
(O'CONOR)

Clonalis, Seat of The O'Conor don. Co. Roscommon, 1972. (Curley)

Front entrance to Dromoland Castle, Newmarket-on-Fergus, County Clare, Seat of Lord Inchiquin, Sir Phaedrig Lucius Ambrose O'Brien. 1972.

IRELAND (O'BRIEN)

BELOW: Lord Inchiquin of Ireland and his wife, Lady Vera.

ABOVE: The late Donough O'Brien, Lord Inchiquin, with his wife, Lady Anne, and their daughters, The Hon. Deirdre O'Brien Chapin and The Hon. Grania O'Brien. Co. Clare, 1966.

LEFT: Lord Terence O'Neill of The Maine. Belfast, 1972. (Leslie Stuart)
RIGHT: Lord O'Neill of Ireland. (Leslie Stuart)

IRELAND (O'NEILL)

ABOVE: Lord O'Neill's residence at Shanes Castle. (Leslie Stuart)

LEFT: Lord and Lady O'Neill with sons, Shane, Tyrone, and Rory. Shanes Castle, Antrim, Northern Ireland. 1972. (Leslie Stuart)

LEFT: His Majesty King Umberto. Portugal, 1966. RIGHT: King Umberto at the time of his engagement. Rome, 1932. (Brown Bros.)

ITALY

King Umberto, Queen Maria Jose, and first-born Princess Maria Pia. Naples, 1934. (Oggi)

King Umberto's third child, Princess Maria Gabriella; her husband, Robert de Balkany; and baby Elizabeth. Lausanne, 1972. (Oggi)

BELOW RIGHT: The claimant's only son, Prince Vittorio Emmanuele and his wife, Marina Doria. Geneva, 1972. (Oggi)

ABOVE: Amedeo, Duke of Aosta and his wife, Royal Princess Claudia of France, shopping in Arezzo, Italy, 1972. (Oggi)

His Royal Highness dom Duarte Nuño, Duke of Braganza. Coimbra, Portugal, 1972. (Finlay)

PORTUGAL

ABOVE: Dom Duarte: solitude at Coimbra Palace, 1972. (Finlay)

RIGHT: The Portuguese claimant at his desk. Coimbra, 1972. (Finlay)

LEFT: King Michael of Rumania and his mother, Queen Elena. Bucharest, 1921. (Culver) RIGHT: King Carol, Crown Prince (now King) Michael, and a new Ford. Rumania, 1932. (Culver)

RUMANIA

LEFT: King Michael, London, 1950. RIGHT: King Michael, London, 1960.

1)   The O'Conor don, the Reverend Charles Denis Mary Joseph
     Anthony O'Conor
     HOUSE OF CONCHOBHAR (Conor)

The O'Conor don, claimant to the ancient throne of Ireland,
is a Jesuit priest, an intellectual of the first order, a gentle man,
and a genuinely memorable personality. Charles Denis Mary
Joseph Anthony O'Conor, who was born in 1906, teaches at Clongowes, the Jesuit college that lies in green, flat country some twenty
miles from Dublin, and that served as the model for the school in
James Joyce's *Portrait of the Artist as a Young Man.* Ian Finlay, a
young Irish photojournalist and former Clongowes student, talked
to the claimant in 1972 and found him well: "I met the O'Conor
don at the college. When I arrived he was hovering at the Castle
door watching for me. He was just as I remembered—the 12 years
since I had last seen him had left no visible mark. The same
ascetic, almost skull-like face, the shy smile, the same unforgettable
laughter, which I think is one of the happiest sounds that I've ever
heard. We talked in his dark, crowded room with 'Fr. C. O'Conor'
painted on the door outside. Here he sleeps and writes and corre-
sponds, surrounded by books and a surprising number of black
coats. He is a man of utter modesty, and of great charm. We
walked around the college, and as he chatted with the boys I was
reminded of his almost child-like good humor. His shy, bird-like
movements and gestures are emphasized by the flowing Jesuit
habit. He is surrounded by a great sense of peace."

It is a touching paradox that this gentle, peaceful philosopher
is the inheritor of a tradition of struggle and violence that characterized the Irish dynastic scene for centuries upon centuries.

The O'Conor don is descended from the first Christian king of
Connacht (a province of Ireland) in the fifth century, and King

Roderic O'Conor, the last Ard Ri (High King or supreme monarch of Ireland, who died in 1198).

The O'Conor don is the only representative in Ireland of the old royal Gaelic families who still own at least a part of their ancestral lands, and is still a Catholic. The *Book of Annalists* claims that the O'Conors are descended from Heremon, one of the sons of Milesius, king of Spain, who invaded Ireland around 300 B.C. Their pedigree can be traced to Feradach the Just, a king of Ireland in the first century. It is believed that no family in Europe can trace their descent through so many generations of legitimate ancestors.[2]

The House of O'Conor reached the crest of its power in the early twelfth century with High King Turlough Mor O'Conor, whose son, Roderic, or Cathal Crovedearg of the Wine Red Hand, was the last High King of Ireland. The Normans arrived during Roderic's reign and ended the High Kingship. The O'Conors, however, remained kings of Connacht until the end of the fourteenth century; their territories and power were steadily decreased as the Norman strength in Ireland increased. Even when the O'Conors were no longer kings, and the head of the house became known as O'Conor don, they continued to be inaugurated with all the old traditional ceremony at the historic inaugural site in Connacht.

By the end of the seventeenth century only a fraction of their lands was held by members of the O'Conor family in County Roscommon in Connacht. Today, only Clonalis, near Castlerea, survives; the Irish Land Commission acquired the other property in the 1930s.

The present O'Conor don has been certified by the Genealogical Office, Dublin, as the direct descendant of Conchobhar, Turlough, and Roderic. His family, through the generations, has consistently maintained its aristocratic position notwithstanding the fact that they remained inflexibly Catholic. Members of the House of O'Conor were always, by tradition, very involved in Irish public affairs. All the O'Conor dons of the nineteenth century were members of Parliament. The present O'Conor don entered the Society of Jesus in 1924. He was appointed chaplain of Magistral Grace, Irish Association of the Sovereign Order of the Knights of Rhodes and Malta in 1943. He then became Provincial (head) of the Jesuits in Ireland. That responsibility passed to a younger man about a decade ago.

The present Clonalis House, seat of the O'Conor claimant, was built in the late 1800s and replaced an earlier house whose ruins are still visible from the main road leading to it. The avenue to the house goes through a grove of trees and curves between green fields to the house itself, which crouches atop a small hill. Miss Josephine O'Conor, sister of the claimant, Reverend Charles O'Conor, S.J., the present head of the family, lives at Clonalis House and represents her brother. She oversees the big, comfortable residence, and is attended by several servants who cook, clean, and tend the lovely flower gardens. Miss Mary Morris, the housekeeper, shows the relics and manuscripts that reflect the battle waged by successive generations of O'Conors to maintain a foothold against the recurrent waves of centuries of foreign rule. Clonalis is the only historic house in Ireland open to the public (during certain months of the year) that represents the *Irish* rather than the *Anglo-Irish* tradition, and illustrates the survival of this tradition from the coming of Christianity to Ireland in the fifth century up to the present day. The history of Clonalis is, in miniature, the history of Ireland.

While all three of the Irish claimants are valid, speculation, which considers the possibility of reestablishing a monarchial representative in Ireland, would have to give the edge to the House of O'Conor. This conclusion must be reached after the realization that today Eire is over 95 percent Catholic, and the Irish historical and sentimental traditions are strongly emphasized. (Northern Ireland is two-thirds Protestant, and has the mixed and contentious historical traditions of the Irish, Scotch-Irish, and English.) The other claims, the House of O'Brien and the House of O'Neill, as represented by the Protestants Lord Inchiquin and Lord O'Neill, would have less appeal to the Celtic center of the average Irish heart.

It is conceivable that a monarchist party could be established in Ireland. For its members to be eligible to stand for election to the Dail (Parliament) as such, a political party must first be registered by appropriate authority. Registration is not easily granted to "mushroom" parties. A body that stood for the creation or restoration of a monarchy would probably not be prohibited by the Constitution from working toward this objective, provided that its policy was to proceed in a constitutional, not a revolutionary, fashion; to work peacefully for a change in the Constitution that could only be effected by a referendum.

The O'Conor don considers the concept of monarchial claimancy in Ireland as totally anachronistic. As a philosopher and a man of God, he undoubtedly views his lineage and his position as a royal claimant as intrusions upon the point of Life, and the purpose of his dedication.

If there were others who disagreed with him—and in Ireland the expected rarely occurs, while the impossible happens with regularity—there *could* be a sentimental rallying to the O'Conor claim for the sake of Irish unity. Should the O'Conor don eschew the call, the claim would pass to his nephews.

2)   The Right Honorable Lord Inchiquin, Seventeenth Baron of Inchiquin, Sir Phaedrig Lucius Ambrose O'Brien, Ninth Baronet of Lemeneagh
HOUSE OF BRIAN BOROIMHE (O'Brien)

The 1970s have been agonizing years for the people of Ireland. Not only did the tensions and tragedies in Northern Ireland (or "Occupied Ireland" as some Anglophobes call it) escalate, but they provoked economic punishments in the form of trade shrinkage, a steep decline in tourism, and a general atmosphere of political malaise and instability. These woes coincided with Great Britain's and (the Republic of) Ireland's prospective entry into the Common Market. Both countries agreed to join, and their admission to the European Community was ratified. Great Britain and Ireland became members of the same new club.

But the bombings, killings, and havoc continued in Northern Ireland, and spilled over sporadically into the Republican south. The questions kept being shouted: When will the Catholics and Protestants in the North stop assassinating each other? Why don't the English get the hell out of the island of Ireland? Why can't a compromise be found?

If the magnetism of compromise attracted the various factions of Ireland, it is conceivably possible that there could be a role to play, in a united Ireland, for another claimant to the ancient Celtic throne—The Right Honorable Lord Inchiquin, Seventeenth Baron of Inchiquin, Sir Phaedrig Lucius Ambrose O'Brien. Lord Inchiquin is the direct male descendant of the Dalcassian [3] King Brian Boru, the Ard Ri (High King or supreme monarch) of Ireland who was slain by the Danes in the eleventh century. Although the O'Briens' High Kingship was subsequently cleaved, they remained the reigning dynasty of Thomond (in the Province of North Munster) until the middle of the sixteenth century.

The O'Briens are also descendants of Milesius, king of Spain, through his sons Heber, Heremon, and Ir, who reputedly led the Milesian invasion of Ireland, and settled there about the time of Alexander the Great. The Milesians established the dynasties of the ruling Gaelic families of Ireland, including the O'Briens, O'Neills, and O'Conors. Lord Inchiquin states that the O'Brien claim is paramount over the O'Conor claim, since the O'Briens are descended most directly from Heber, the third son of King Milesius, while the O'Conors are from the junior branch of Heremon, Milesius's eighth son. Memories in Ireland are known to be long; it is stunning to consider that events of thirty-seven hundred years ago still have a bearing on current views.[4]

The House of O'Brien has great and strong roots back to the Roman Catholic tradition, but has been Protestant since the beginning of the eighteenth century. Indeed, it is one of the few native Gaelic houses now in the English peerage.

Sir Phaedrig Lucius Ambrose O'Brien, the Right Honorable Lord Inchiquin, succeeded his brother, Donough, to the title and claim in 1968. He was born in April 1900, and was educated at Eton, Magdalen College, Oxford M.A.) and Imperial College, London University.

As a younger son with no family expectations, the present Lord Inchiquin went to Africa in 1922, where he worked until 1959, with interruptions by World War II. Inchiquin ran a flourishing coffee plantation in Kenya, worked in the gold fields of east and central Africa, prospected in Uganda and the Congo, and was appointed to the staff of the Anglo-American Corporation of South Africa. Lord Inchiquin was a major with the British East African Intelligence Corps and was wounded in the Abyssinian campaign. In 1945 he married Vera, the daughter of Reverend Clifton S.

Winter of Devon, England. The heir presumptive is Lord Inchiquin's younger (sixty-eight) brother, Fionn Myles Maryous O'Brien, who was in the British Royal Air Force in World War II and lives in London. Fionn has a son, Conor.

The present head of the House of O'Brien takes great interest in his position as head of the ancient family of O'Brien and pays close attention to the management of the Inchiquin Settled Estates at Dromoland. The O'Brien's seat was and is Dromoland Castle near Newmarket-on-Fergus, County Clare—about twenty minutes by car from Shannon Airport. In the mid-1940s the former claimant, Donough O'Brien, Lord Inchiquin, and his wife, Lady Inchiquin, the former Honorable Anne Molyneux Thesiger, the daughter of Viscount Chelmsford, rufurbished the castle and, to help defray the rising costs of maintenance, agreed to accept recommended paying guests during certain months of each year. The late claimant, Donough, and his late wife have two daughters—the Honorable Dierdre J. F. O'Brien Chapin, the wife of a New York physician, and the Honorable Grania O'Brien Weir who worked as social secretary for the British ambassadors in Peru and Tokyo, and later for Mrs. John Hay Whitney, the wife of the former United States Ambassador to the Court of St. James.

Ever-increasing expenses and taxes forced Donough in 1962, with the consent of the trustees, to sell the castle, and a portion of its expansive acreage to an American, West Virginia businessman Bernard McDonough, who has turned the castle and a portion of the property into one of Ireland's most famous hotels. A new family residence, Thomond House, was then built on a hill overlooking the castle. Over the rolling pastures of Dromoland, where generations of royal O'Briens trod, there are the bridle paths and walks which were made by Sir Edward O'Brien about two hundred fifty years ago, and now a new eighteen-hole golf course. The castle still has a remarkable collection of O'Brien portraits and memorabilia.

Lord and Lady Inchiquin have had long family connections with both Ireland and England: Lady Vera is descended from an old Saxon Catholic family in the middle ages, and on her mother's side is related to the O'Neills. The Dromoland O'Briens, now the senior branch, lived in Lemeneagh Castle, twenty miles northwest of Dromoland, in the sixteenth and seventeenth centuries, until the Cromwellian invasion of Ireland, when Lord Inchiquin's ancestor, Conor O'Brien, was killed in 1651 defending his land and castle against the invaders. Conor's son, Donough, was sent to England to be brought up as a Protestant. When Donough later returned to his Irish estates, however, he supported the Catholic cause of King James II against William of Orange, and was created a baronet by James.

Donough O'Brien's son married a first cousin of the English queens Mary and Anne, thus establishing a connection with the English royal family through the last two reigning members of the House of Stuart. Donough's widowed mother, Moira, a Catholic, was able to save the vast O'Brien estates in County Clare by marrying a Protestant English army officer.

In spite of more recent English connections, the O'Briens have struggled continuously to maintain their Irish inheritance. From 1582, when an earlier Donough O'Brien was executed by order of Queen Elizabeth I for opposing her conquest of Ireland, to less than a hundred and fifty years ago when William Smith O'Brien, a famous patriot and great-great-great-uncle of the current claimant, was found guilty of high treason by the British, the O'Briens have fought for their Irish tradition.

Although the title of Baron Inchiquin is an English creation (but an Irish peerage), if Irish royalism found some traction and support, there is no question that Sir Phaedrig Lucius O'Brien, amateur historian, archaeologist, and genealogist, as a descendant of King Brian Boru, would receive consideration. Perhaps a claimant with bloodlines on both sides of the Irish Sea has distinct appeal for those interested in an ultimate solution to the anguished Anglo-Irish problems.

3) Fourth Baron O'Neill, Lord Raymond Arthur Clanaboy O'Neill
HOUSE OF UI NIALL (O'Neill)

The O'Neill claimant succeeded his father, the third baron, who was killed in action with the British forces in Italy during World War II. Lord O'Neill was born in 1933, was married at thirty to Georgina Mary, the elder daughter of Lord Francis John Montagu Douglas Scott of London, who is the brother of the duchess of Gloucester. They have three sons: Shane, Tyrone, and Rory.

Lord O'Neill has a very British cut, but with an overlay of Irishness. The eyes, the face, the manner echo a Celtic strain. The O'Neills live at Shanes Castle in County Antrim, Northern Ireland (Ulster) and, part of the year, in London. O'Neill went to Eton, the Royal Agricultural College in Cirencester, England, and was a major in the North Irish Horse Regiment, a volunteer reserve force, until late 1971.

The life style of the O'Neills at Shanes Castle can be envied by almost all the other European claimants. The O'Neills are not suffering from a lack of funds. Like the O'Conor don, Lord O'Neill sees the Irish claimancy as rather capricious; he is not hounded by the stringencies of his position as claimant or pretender. Lord and Lady O'Neill are respected and admired; they are involved in farming, forestry, business, sports, and cultural affairs, and have no regal axe to grind. Their style of living has been described as the Life of Reilly—but Raymond O'Neill says that he does "not think it is possible for anybody in Northern Ireland to live the life of that gentleman at the present time. . . ."

Raymond O'Neill's principal interests are centered in Northern Ireland where, apart from running a farming and forestry enterprise at Shanes Castle, he is a director of an automobile distribution company and an insurance firm. Lord O'Neill is also actively involved in a number of charitable and philanthropic projects dealing with youth and conservation. He is also an *aficionado* of old motor cars and trains; he operates a narrow-gauge railway at Shanes Castle, which is open to the public during the summer.

Shanes Castle is only about twenty miles from Belfast—but it is light-years away from the depressing urban atmosphere that envelopes most of the capital of Northern Ireland. Lord O'Neill's house lies along the shores of Lough Neagh, the largest lake in the British Isles—virtually an inland sea. The river Maine flows through the park of the estate. The old Shanes Castle was burned down by accident in 1816. The elegance, splendor, beauty, and enchantment that characterized life at Shanes Castle several centuries ago is still reflected there today. After the fire the O'Neills converted the extensive stables to living quarters, and over the years, built other additions. A relatively recent addition (1860) was also burned—but accidentally—by the Sinn Feiners during the time of the troubles in 1922. When Raymond O'Neill returned to Shanes Castle in the early 1950s, there was no house to speak of on the estate. His father did not live at Shanes Castle very much, and no attempt had been made to replace the house destroyed fifty years ago. Lord O'Neill built a Georgian house on the property, which was completed in 1958.

Burke's Peerage, which devotes over twenty thousand words to the O'Neill family, says: "The great dynastic House of O'Neill is the most famous branch of the royal family of Tara, whose recorded filiation is accepted by scholars from about A.D. 360 and which is the oldest traceable family in Europe." This conflicts with the O'Conor ancestoral traceability, which goes back to A.D. 75. (The family of the Russian claimant's wife—the Georgian/Armenian House of Bagration-Moukhransky—is probably the oldest of the royal *Christian* dynasties. The O'Conor and O'Neill kings of Ireland were Druidic in the early generations before Saint Patrick started his mission of conversion to Christ in the fifth century.) The O'Neill claimant is the descendant of King Niall of "The Nine Hostages" who lived fifteen hundred years ago and asserted at least nominal suzerainty over the whole island of Ireland—a High King. The O'Neills provided High Kings to Ireland from the fifth century until the thirteenth century, and reigned as provincial kings in Northern Ireland from 425 until 1603.[5]

There is an immeasurable difference today between the life of the aesthetic Jesuit who represents the O'Conor claim, and the stylish aristocrat who is the O'Neill claimant. But they are related. King Niall Ruadh (The Red), king of Ulster in 1230, was married to the daughter of King Cathal O'Conor of Connacht (1201–1224) and produced a son Brian whose progeny carry both bloods. The O'Conor-O'Neill-O'Brien families represent a fascinatingly ancient royal legitimacy that can challenge any of their Continental counterparts on the score of antiquity and traceability.

The Irish claimants are very cavalier and unconcerned about their position—strikingly unlike the other crownless Europeans. There is, however, a strange, cogent, and very relevant twist to the Irish claimancy and prospects. Lord O'Neill's uncle is viewed by some people as a possible cog in a compromise solution to Ireland's current bloody hiatus between the north and the south. He is Lord Terence O'Neill of the Maine, former prime minister of Northern Ireland.

In late 1971 there was a well-founded rumor that the president

of the Republic, the legendary Eamon de Valera, met privately
in Dublin with the ousted prime minister—a moderate, an aristocrat, and a Protestant (Church of Ireland, which is Anglican), who
is now a partner in the London merchant banking firm of S. G.
Warburg & Co. De Valera is reputed to have said that, at ninety
years of age and *almost* blind, he still hopes to live long enough
to see at least the dim outline of a compromise in the form of a
united Ireland whose first president would be Lord O'Neill of the
Maine.[6]

This is not a thin thought. Terence O'Neill is a practiced par-
liamentarian; he is in his fifties, vibrant, warm, bright, and interested in getting back into government. On the basis of merit and
by a process of elimination, Terence O'Neill of the Maine could
become again a prime mover in Irish politics. He has already been,
in the Northern Ireland government, high sheriff, M.P. for twenty-
four years, parliamentary secretary, minister of health, deputy
speaker, and officer in the Irish Guards, minister of home affairs,
minister of finance, and finally, for six years, prime minister. If
Terence O'Neill could get the top job in a new Ireland, it would
mean that the ancient royal Celtic blood was back in the business
of running the country—an art and a practice that this family exercised for a millenium.

NOTES

1. The exclusion of the Irish claim from royalty-watching exercises is
easily understood if one considers the English political necessity over the
years to obliterate such claims. There is also an even more pragmatic reason:
family relationships. With the exception of Albania and Turkey, all of the
European royal families are very *closely* related—present sovereigns and
claimants. The Irish royal lines are not, for all practical purposes, related to
the others. However, this is not precisely accurate: The houses of O'Conor,
O'Brien, and O'Neill have definite connections with various royal dynasties
of England, Scotland, France, Spain, and Portugal—particularly the O'Neills
and the O'Briens. Genealogists can trace the ancient royal Irish lines back

to the pre-Christian centuries; from those days, shrouded in the Celtic mist, up to the Middle Ages, there were many intermarriages and family connections with the Continental and British reigning houses. But today it would be stretching a point for any of the Irish claimants to call their European peers "cousins."

2. GENEALOGICAL TABLE OF THE HOUSE OF O'CONOR

1. Feredach the Just RH *	c.75	32. Cathal RC	1010
2. Fiacha Finnola RH	c.95	33. Teige of the White Steed RC	1030
3. Tuathal Techmar RH	c.130	34. Hugh of the Broken Spar RC	1067
4. Felim the Lawgiver	c.164	35. Roderic (Rory of the Yellow	
5. Conn of the 100 Battles RH	c.177	Hound) RC	1105
6. Art the Solitary RH	c.195	36. Turlough Mor O'Conor RH	1156
7. Cormac RH	c.227	37. Cathal Crovedearg RC	1224
8. Cairbre Liffechair RH	284	38. Hugh RC	1228
9. Fiacha Straiftene RH	322	39. Roderick (Rory) (Never King)	1244
10. Murchertagh Fireach RH	356	40. Owen RC	1274
11. Eochy Moymedon RH	366	41. Hugh RC	1309
12. Bryan RC **	397	42. Turlough RC	1345
13. Duagh Galach RC	438	43. Hugh RC	1356
14. Eoghan Shreve (Never King)	464	44. Turlough Oge (First O'Conor	
15. Muiredhach Mal (Never King)	489	don)	1406
16. Fergus RC	517	45. Felim Geancach	1474
17. Eochy Termacherna RC	543	46. Owen Gaech	1485
18. Hugh (Aedh) RC	577	47. Carbry	1546
19. Uada RC	599	48. Dermot	1585
20. Roghallach RC	645	49. Sir Hugh	1632
21. Fergus RC	649	50. Cahill Oge	1634
22. Muiredhach Muilethan RC	700	51. Charles	1696
23. Innrechtach (Enright) RC	751	52. Denis	1750
24. Muirgis (Never King)	774	53. Charles	1790
25. Tomaltach (Never King)	810	54. Denis	1804
26. Muirgis RC	723	55. Owen MP	1831
27. Teige (Never King)	841	56. Denis MP	1847
28. Concover (Conor) RC	879	57. Charles Owen MP	1905
29. Cathal RC	925	58. Denis Charles	1917
30. Teige of the Three Towers RC	954	59. Owen	1943
31. Conor RC	971	60. Charles Reverend, SJ Now Living	

* RH Rex Hiberniae (king of Ireland)
** RC Rex Connachtia (king of Connacht)

3. "Dalcassian." Dal Cas was the tribe, clan, or sept of which Brian was the head.

4. My own family, through my father's mother, are the O'Gradys of Kilballyowen, one of the most ancient in North Munster (Thomond), who had a common ancestry with the O'Briens. The O'Briens, however, in the person of Brian Boru, subsequently established an ascendant power in Thomond, over which they became hereditary rulers. The O'Gradys acknowledged the

O'Briens' paramount sway and were arrayed as dynasts, or chiefs of a sept, under the banners of the O'Brien provincial princes.

My cousin, Gerald de Courcey The O'Grady, lives today with his wife and young daughters on the lands of Kilballyowen that the family acquired in 1309 and that have since remained the principal residence and seat of The O'Grady. Kilballyowen is near Bruff, County Limerick, about twenty miles from Limerick City.

The Kilballyowen O'Gradys, in order to preserve their lands and primacy, conformed to Protestantism at the time of Henry VIII. Centuries later, in the 1840s, my O'Grady great-grandmother married a Catholic, John Deere, became a Catholic, and, reputedly because of family pressures, moved to the United States with my grandmother as a babe-in-arms. Apparently, the only acknowledgment of the old connection was upon the birth of my father, who was christened Waller (since euphemized to "Walter") in memory of my grandmother's kinsman, the Honorable Waller O'Grady of Castlegarde, who was Queen's Counsel in Limerick in the late eighteenth century.

The last echo of the family religious differences occurred in 1963 when my father took his three American sisters to call on The O'Grady at Kilballyowen. One sister, from California, was in her late seventies, the others, from Pennsylvania, not far behind. They went with Gerald O'Grady to visit the small family church in the village of Knockaney near Bruff—replete with O'Grady memorabilia. As the sisters sat in the hushed and empty church on a lonely afternoon, the eldest was heard to say, in a hissing whisper, after she had peered around and noticed the Anglican trappings: "My God! I think that great-grandpapa was a *Protestant!*"

Celtic minds have long memories on many scores.

5. To be totally accurate about "The O'Neill," the literal—if not actual —O'Neill claimant is Jorge, The O'Neill of Clanaboy, chief of his ancient and royal name, and recognized by the genealogical office in Dublin as heir male of the last "properly inaugurated Prince of Clanaboy, senior branch of the old Royal House of Ulster." The paradox, however, is that Jorge The O'Neill is a Portuguese nobleman as his predecessors have been for generations.

Jorge The O'Neill is, in the words of Lord Raymond O'Neill, the "accepted" head. The O'Brien claimant, Lord Inchiquin, says that "The O'Neills could have had an equal claim with the O'Briens, but they left Ireland after the Cromwellian wars, and the Head of the O'Neill Family now lives in Portugal as a Portuguese. . . ."

Jorge O'Neill, who is sixty-five years old, lives on Rua da Junqueira 10, Lisbon, and also on the old family estate in Setubal, Portugal. Jorge married an Italo-Portuguese noblewoman, dona Josefina-Luisa Ricciardi-Roquette, and has four daughters and two sons, the oldest of whom, Hugo 37 is the heir apparent to the name.

The O'Neills fought against the British in Ireland in the seventeenth century, and joined the "Flight of the Earls" in 1607. Again, when Jorge's direct ancestor, Felim, fought against William of Orange as a Jacobite officer at the Battle of the Boyne in 1690, and was defeated, The O'Neill fled to France to serve the French monarchy. The O'Neills took with them the ancient royal blood which the Continental dynasts understand so well. It was not surprising to find, eventually, the old Celtic royal line being readily assimilated—and sought by—the somewhat inbred royal houses of Europe.

On Jorge O'Neill's grandmother's side of the family, they are directly related to King John VI of Portugal (1816–1826) and emperor of Brazil (1816–1822). The O'Neills of Portugal are of the most pristinely aristocratic. Their bloodlines, since the 1600s, have been intertwined with the oligarchic and political fabric of the Iberian Peninsula. Jorge's brother, Fernando, married the daughter of the late Joao Franco, prime minister and dictator of Portugal (1906–08). His uncle, Henry, was the Portuguese minister of justice. The O'Neills of Portugal, from the time of their arrival on the Continent, have been sprinkled with honors, noble prerogatives, and basic social power.

The Portuguese O'Neills—codescendants of the Milesians with the O'Conors and the O'Briens—almost close a final loop: We say that all the royal houses of Europe are closely related with the exception of Albania, Ireland, and Turkey. The ancient Irish royal lines are fundamentally and ultimately connected with the English, Scottish, Portuguese, and Spanish bloods—which leaves only the Albanian and the Turkish claimants "unconnected."

6. Irish paradox asserted itself in May 1973. The vastly Roman Catholic electorate of the Republic voted in as president a sixty-eight year old Protestant who in looks and manner would make an excellent member of the British House of Lords—Mr. Erskine Childers. Colin Frost of The *New York Post* said: "The Irish Presidency is not an executive job, but sort of an elected monarchy, and Erskine Childers has the style to go with it."

The new president's father, Erskine Childers, was an English army officer who took up the Irish cause and sided with Eamon de Valera in the civil war of 1922-23. The elder Childers was captured, sentenced to death, and executed by the Irish Free State government of William T. Cosgrave (irony wrapped in paradox), father of the Republic of Ireland's present and newly elected prime minister, Liam Cosgrave.

THE KINGDOM OF ITALY

His Majesty King Umberto II
HOUSE OF SAVOY

The Italian government, in the autumn of 1972, made an official request to its citizens that they refrain from sending Christmas cards because of the strike-ridden, tumultuous condition of the postal department. This confusion was only another straw on a huge bundle of woes that had beset many aspects of the Italian scene: strikes in airlines, hotels, restaurants, trains, taxis; monetary crisis, inflation, mercurial political balances, reactionary Vatican pronouncements, and a general feeling of frustration at all levels.

Claudio Mazzaro, who works in a haberdashery in the arcade of Piazza Castello in Turin, said to an American visitor in 1971: "That is the Palazzo del Principe di Savoia across the way. I wouldn't mind at all if King Umberto were there in residence. It was probably better a hundred years or so ago when we had the Kingdom of Savoy, and to the devil with the rest of Italy. I don't care if it sounds old-fashioned. We were better off with Kings. Things worked better. They were good to watch. Even when they moved to Rome, and even when we had Mussolini, we still had little King Victor Emmanuel. The royal family are from Turin, you know. With all these strikes, taxes, and bad business, why is it such a bad idea to bring the King back? Why? It can be no worse."

King Umberto, the claimant to the crown of Italy, agrees completely. He would like the job. His family have been at this sort of
work since the eleventh century. They ran the Piedmont area of
Italy, Cyprus, Armenia, Jerusalem, Sicily, Sardinia, and eventually
a unified Italy. His family's connections and bloodlines run
through all the royal families of Europe. Umberto himself did
have the job, but lost it after only one month. He has been trying
very seriously ever since to get it back.

His Majesty King Umberto was born in the Chateau Racconigi
near Turin in the Piedmont in 1904. He is the third child and
only son of King Victor Emmanuel III of Italy and his queen,
the former Princess Helena Petrovich Niegoch of Montenegro.
Umberto was regent of the Kingdom for two years, and was proclaimed king on May 9, 1946, when the Allied Powers requested
that his father abdicate. His reign was short: After a plebiscite
which gave a small majority—12.7 million against 10.7 million—to
the Republic in June 1946, King Umberto was forced into exile
a week later without renouncing any of his sovereign rights nor
abdicating. Upon ex-King Victor Emmanuel's death in Egypt in
1947, Umberto became the sole, legitimate head of the House of
Savoy.

In Rome on January 8, 1930, Umberto was married to Princess
Maria-José of Belgium, daughter of King Albert I of Belgium and
Queen Elizabeth, the former duchess-in-Bavaria. Umberto's sister,
Queen Giovanna, was the wife of the late king of Bulgaria, Boris
III, and the mother of the Bulgarian claimant, King Simeon.

Umberto and Maria-José have four children: Princess Maria
Pia (thirty-seven) who married Prince Alexander of Yugoslavia,
the son of Prince Paul of Yugoslavia and Princess Olga of Greece
and Denmark; Crown Prince Victor Emmanuel, Prince of Naples
(thirty-five); Princess Maria Gabriella (thirty-two); and Princess
Maria-Beatrice (twenty-nine).

King Umberto is a spare and elegant man of sixty-nine. He lives in a comfortable villa in Cascais on the coast of Portugal. The king and his wife, Queen Maria-José, have lived quietly apart for most of the past twenty years. The queen lives in Switzerland. Umberto has substantial holdings in England, and can be considered financially well off. He is attended by a quasi—court in exile and devotes a major part of his time to political and social matters relative to his position as former monarch and head of the House of Savoy.

The claimant to the Italian throne is beset by several factors—both historical and current, political and personal—which are peculiar to the Italian scene. Italy has a recognized and active monarchist party, which, ironically, the king does not support; Italy has the largest Communist party in Europe west of the Iron Curtain; and the immediate family of the claimant have not provided a public image that is calculated to endear them to their fellow countrymen.

In the May 1972 national elections in Italy, the neo-Fascist Italian Social Movement, allied with the declining Monarchist party in a new national right wing, retained the gains it won in Sicily, other parts of southern Italy, and Rome in the local elections of June 1971. The small Monarchist party, however, (P.D.I.U.M.—*Partito Democratico Italiano di Unita Monarchica*) has never had the support of Umberto or of the leading Monarchists, who believe that the monarchy should be above politics. The principal monarchist organization in Italy, the Italian Monarchial Union (U.M.I.—*Unione Monarchica Italiana*) has the support of the king, members of many other political parties, and reputedly a membership of eight hundred and fifty thousand. The U.M.I. is, in turn, affiliated with the Young Monarchist Front (F.M.G.—*Fronte Monarchica Giovanile*), which cooperates in organizing meetings, publishing manifestos and royal messages, and generally coordinating monarchist movements in Italy. King Umberto works closely with the latter two organizaitons.

But the claimant's viability is continually corroded by the vagaries of his own children: The Heir Apparent, Crown Prince Victor Emmanuel, has compounded the weakness of his dynastic standing by marrying an Italian commoner, Miss Marina Doria, in Las Vegas, Nevada, in 1970, with a second ceremony in Teheran, Iran, in 1971, after several years of well-publicized companionship (Victor Emmanuel and Marina had their first child, Emmanuel Filiberto, in Geneva in July 1972); Princess Maria Pia is divorced from Prince Alexander of Yugoslavia; Princess Maria Gabriella was married in 1969 to a rich, divorced Hungarian-Rumanian financier, Robert de Balkany; and the youngest child, Princess Maria-Beatrice, married an Argentine diplomat after various escapades and romances with types not designed to amuse royalist sympathizers—nor the Vatican.

In spite of these liabilities and burdens, King Umberto survives as the head of the royal house and as a legitimate claimant. He is encouraged by the fact that the Italian monarchist associations are the most active in any of the European republics. Although lacking the endorsement of the claimant himself, in May 1972 the Italian Monarchist party elected 5 (out of 630) members to the Chamber of Deputies, and 4 (out of 322) members to the Senate.

There is, too, the fact that Umberto is a level-headed, legally trained, attractive personality who has maintained his dignity and his dedication in the face of great personal challenges. The House of Savoy is also fortunate to have as its prospective spokesman, Umberto's nephew, His Royal Highness Amedeo, duke of Aosta. Amedeo is twenty-eight years old, personable, active in the Italian Monarchial Union, and very popular. He is married to Her Royal Highness Princess Claude, daughter of the Count of Paris, claimant to the French throne. The Duke and Duchess of Aosta live in the countryside of Arezzo, Italy, with their son and two daughters.

While it is not probable that the recent and unexpectedly strong showing (40 percent of the popular vote) by the Christian Democrat party will be soon challenged, it is not at all impossible to conceive of a resurgence of royalist sympathies in Italy, where feelings are volatile and romantic traditions run deep. His Majesty King Umberto could play the claimant's ace by remaining the head of the royal house but designating his nephew as the claimant. Such a move might give the Italian Monarchist movement a needed transfusion of credibility, and increase immeasurably the possibility of a return of the House of Savoy to the throne of Italy.

THE KINGDOM OF PORTUGAL

His Royal Highness dom Duarte Nuño, Duke of Braganza
HOUSE OF BRAGANZA

Of all the currently crownless royal persons, the Portuguese claimant may be the one who provokes the most sympathy in the royalty-watcher. Solitary, gentle, and kind, this descendant of French kings and head of the royal house that ruled Portugal for over eight hundred years lives quietly—almost timidly—in the country several hours by car north of Lisbon. Ian Finlay met twice with His Royal Highness dom Duarte Nuño, duke of Braganza, in the spring of 1972.

"I was apprehensive about my meeting with dom Duarte," said Finlay, "because don Juan of Spain had told me that, since the death of dom Duarte's wife a couple of years ago, he has suffered from nervous depression. When I met him first, it was at his sister's house in Lisbon—a small, rather gloomy place. On both occasions, in Lisbon and later in Coimbra, he appeared carrying the same small transistor radio.

"We talked exclusively in German which he speaks with a strong Austrian accent. He is very shy, self-effacing, and immensely courteous—with the manner and style of an old-fashioned aristocrat. For me he had great charm. It was very strange to see him again in Coimbra—a small, bothered man completely lost in an enormous, empty palace. Apart from one maid, dom Duarte lives utterly alone. I stayed with him for most of the afternoon and he seemed delighted to have someone to talk to. With great pride he showed me his cactus collection—he had started with only two a few years ago, and now has a family of almost fifty. It tugged my heart. The Duke and the Cactus: it would make a sad short-story. . . ."

Dom Duarte Nuño was born in Austria in 1907. He is the eighth child of Prince dom Miguel and of the former Princess de Lowenstein-Wertheim-Rosenberg, his second wife. After the renunciation of rights in 1920 by his eldest brother, dom Miguel, who had married morganatically, and upon the death of Manuel II in 1932 in England, dom Duarte was recognized as His Majesty King Duarte by the Portuguese monarchist groups and royalist movements. He was married in Brazil in 1942 to his cousin, the Royal Princess Françoise of Orléans and Braganza, the sister of the Countess of Paris, who is the wife of the Bourbon-Orléans claimant to the French throne. Princess Françoise was the great-granddaughter of dom Pedro, emperor of Brazil. Their marriage united two branches of the Portuguese royal house.

Dom Duarte and Princess Françoise have three sons, dom Duarte-Joao (twenty-seven), dom Miguel (twenty-six), and dom Henrique-Joao (twenty-three), all of whom were born in Berne, Switzerland. Princess Françoise died in 1970.

Dom Duarte lives virtually alone in San Marcos palace in Coimbra, Portugal. Before returning to his homeland, he and his family lived in Switzerland. Death would have been the penalty had dom Duarte put a foot into Portugal. When the throne was lost in 1910, all the Braganza properties were confiscated—possibly illegally. The law which enforced the royal family's exile was abrogated in 1950. This action may be interpreted as meaning that the present Portuguese government no longer feels that a royalist resurgence is possible. Some observers feel, however, that there is substantial latent sympathy for the monarchy and that the government might even restore the crown with the understanding that the royal family must reciprocate political support. This was probably a more valid view while Salazar was running Portugal. There was some belief that Salazar might consider making a move toward a return of the monarchy somewhat as Franco has done in Spain. It is generally agreed that about 20 percent of the population is openly pro-monarchy—and that many more are sympathetic.

Monarchist sentiment among the Portuguese raises its head in strange and unexpected ways. For example, in August 1972, Portugal made a gesture that was at once ghoulish and tasteful. As *Newsweek* Magazine reported: "To help its former colony celebrate its sequicentennial, the Portuguese Government exhumed the bones of Dom Pedro I, Brazil's first Emperor, and shipped them back to Rio de Janeiro. There, the relics have gone on a nationwide tour that has drawn tens of thousands of worshipful spectators. Eventually, Pedro's remains will join those of other royal family members whose bones have been painstakingly reassembled over the past 51 years. But the Brazilians have one complaint: Pedro's heart remains in Portugal, preserved in formaldehyde."

Dom Duarte is a father-figure to the monarchists; he is, indeed, *de jure* King Duarte (Edward) II of Portugal. He is a courtly, impoverished, and charming man; he lives with the idea of regaining the sovereignty, but he views his position as one of duty and obligation if he is called. Duty, family duty, are important words to dom Duarte. He takes the monarchial position and its implication quite literally and seriously. (*See* Interview, p. 151.) He feels that monarchy offers his people security and continuity. Expedience and political maneuvering run against the grain of the Portuguese claimant. He believes, for example, that Franco has tarnished the fundamental principle of monarchy and succession by passing over don Juan for the throne of Spain in favor of his son, Prince Juan-Carlos. In dom Duarte's book, these rules cannot be twisted for mere political reasons. Dom Duarte thinks dynastically. The heir to the Portuguese royal house, Prince dom Duarte-Joao, the eldest son, is unmarried. His father feels, in accordance with the rules (and in agreement with almost all other claimants), that he must marry someone from a noble family so that the breeding succession can be controlled.

His Royal Highness, the duke of Braganza, is a passive rallying point for the royalists; he does not push his case. It would be difficult for him to do as a resident of Portugal. He would find his life and purpose fulfilled, however, if the House of Braganza were restored. Such a move is not inconceivable. A restored crown in Spain does not at all hurt dom Duarte's cause in Portugal—even if a royal rule was bent to accomplish it.

THE KINGDOM OF RUMANIA

His Majesty King Michael I
HOUSE OF HOHENZOLLERN-SIGMARINGEN

On November 9, 1945, the following item appeared in the London *Times:* "Bucharest. Communist attempts to break up a mass demonstration in front of the royal palace here today, on the occasion of King Michael's birthday, led to serious disorders, in which it is estimated that six persons were killed. A crowd estimated at between 40,000 and 50,000 gathered in the square early shouting 'Long live the king!' Soon afterwards about 15 lorries and buses, loaded with Communists who were giving the clenched fist salute and shouting 'Long live the Groza government!' and other Communist slogans, drove among the crowd, trying to break it up. The crowd overturned two lorries and set them ablaze. The other lorries then withdrew. After Rumanian troops had fired on the demonstrators, General Susaikov, Russian commanding officer in Bucharest and head of the Allied Control Commission, intervened."

King Michael was twenty-five years old at the time, and still sitting precariously on the throne of Rumania amidst the desperate struggle between the traditionalists and the Communists. Two years later he was gone, the throne relegated to museum status, and the Red Star flew over Rumania's ninety-two thousand square miles and twenty million people. Balkan politics had had another upheaval, and the head of the House of Hohenzollern-Sigmaringen moved into exile to fight his cause.

Elements of this royal family ruled Prussia and principalities of the Holy Roman Empire for many centuries. King Michael has in his veins the blood of the royal houses of Prussia, Greece, and Denmark, and is, like almost every other claimant, a cousin of both Queen Elizabeth of England and Prince Philip. He is tenacious and staunch in the Germanic fashion; he has a melancholy that Shakespeare found so untypically preeminent in the Dane of Elsinore, and he bears paradoxically in his face the traces of a certain Mediterranean sensuousness. In his heart he carries the glowing, if dimmed, hope of wearing again the crown of Rumania.

King Michael I of Rumania was born in the Chateau de Foischor in Sinaïa in 1921, the only son of King Carol II and Queen Helena, the former royal princess of Greece and Denmark. Until 1951 there was a unique technical twist to the claims of Rumania's exiled monarchs. Both were legitimate and both claimants had been kings—Carol and his son Michael. In 1927, upon the death of his grandfather, King Ferdinand I, Michael was proclaimed king of Rumania under a regency—his father, Carol, having left the country during an internal crisis the same year. In 1930 Carol, who had lived in France, returned to Rumania and took the power. He was proclaimed king under the name of Carol II, while Michael became hereditary prince with titles of Grand Voivode of Rumania and duke of Alba-Julia. In 1940 Carol, who had opposed the Nazis, was forced by them to abdicate in favor of Michael, who became once more king of Rumania.

The suave and likable King Carol died twenty years ago at sixty-one. Carol was first married to, and subsequently divorced by, Queen Helena, Princess of Greece, Michael's mother, and later married his "companion" of many years, the red-haired and volup-

tuous Mme. Magda Lupescu, (later titled Princess Helen of Rumania). From 1940 Carol and Magda lived luxuriously in Mexico
City, Rio de Janiero, Havana, and in Estoril, where she still lives.
Carol sent a great deal of his wealth out of Rumania to Mme
Lupescu during the 1930s. They lived more lavishly than any of
their royal Estoril neighbors, but were social outcasts among
Carol's peers because of Magda. Carol spent his time listening to
his immense collection of phonograph records, collecting rare
stamps, and shooting pigeons at a local club.

Michael's position during World War II was extremely difficult.
He firmly opposed the Germans and eventually fought against
them with the Russians. After the war, Michael continued to occupy the Rumanian throne despite internal strife. Finally, he, too,
was forced, in December 1947, to abdicate—this time by the Communists.

King Michael was married in 1948 at the age of twenty-seven
in the royal palace in Athens to Her Royal Highness Anne of
Bourbon-Parma, twenty-five, who was born in Paris, the daughter
of Prince René of Bourbon-Parma and Princess Marguerite, a
royal princess of Denmark. Michael and Anne, his third cousin,
met at the wedding of Queen Elizabeth and the Duke of Edinburgh. King Michael and Queen Anne have four daughters: Princess Marguerite (twenty-three), Princess Helena (twenty-two), Princess Irene (twenty), and Princess Sophie (fifteen). Michael and
Anne must have had moments—delicious and poignant—when they
went to London in 1972 for the twenty-fifth wedding anniversary
of Queen Elizabeth and Prince Philip.

King Michael I and Queen Anne live in a villa on Route de
Lausanne, Versoix, Switzerland. Michael has a strong and serious
personality not untouched by a quality of sadness. Some observers
believe that the king feels that life to date—at least political life—

has been a very bitter cup of tea. Michael may feel, with a certain justification, that he was betrayed by his allies.

In spite of his German blood and close Prussian family ties, Michael was firmly anti-Nazi during Hitler's rise to power, and ultimately defied the Axis by fighting the Germans and supporting the Allies. In the postwar political shambles, Michael kept his crown for a few years, but was finally removed by the U.S.S.R., who installed a puppet Communist regime—all presumably with the support and agreement of the British and the Americans.

Michael of Rumania is a businessman. He represents several European and American forms—principally Lockheed Aircraft— and travels each year to various countries on their behalf. Although his father, King Carol, had fled with his substantial treasure fairly intact, it is difficult to know how much of it has flowed, or trickled, down to Michael. It is probable that Michael received a good inheritance from several sides of his family, that Queen Anne also has a modest fortune, and that Michael's business activities and investments produce a comfortable income.

Michael is not insensitive to his position as claimant. (He is, incidentally, the only claimant who declined to discuss his position.) In fact, he views himself as King Michael I of the Rumanians, forced to abdicate, forced to live in exile, but available for recall. He spends a substantial amount of time in correspondence with fellow exiles, and in quiet political discussion with close friends. Michael is not a firebrand exile. This posture and attitude may be appropriate for his business position.

Rumania today, while distinctly Communist and pressed by Russian influence for a generation, has been chafing under the pressures; the Rumanians, by very adroit diplomacy, have begun to reassert their own individuality. In 1972 in Helsinki, at the European Security Conference conceived by the Soviet Union to ratify the post-World War II division of Europe, the Rumanians' defiant role caused a sensation—and considerable embarrassment among her communist allies. Rumania sought to prevent the major powers from dominating the conference, and insisted that the equality, sovereignty, and independence of all nations, big and small, be scrupulously recognized. Any defiance of Russia—which takes the form of independent views and a rediscovered sense of national identity—is fuel for the banked fires of King Michael's ambitions.

The shouts of "Long live the King!" in Bucharest twenty-five years ago, are still ringing in Michael's ears. King Michael was exceptionally popular among his people during the ten years preceding his abdication. There were rumors a few years ago that the king was in touch with a purposeful underground movement in Rumania that fervently wants his return. There is some reason to believe that a free Rumanian election might result in Michael's returning to the throne that he served so well.

RUSSIA

RIGHT: Their Imperial Highnesses Grand Duke Vladimir and Grand Duchess Leonide. Madrid, 1971.

ABOVE: His Imperial Highness Grand Duke Vladimir Cyrilovitch Romanoff. Madrid, 1968. (*The New York Times*)

RIGHT: The Heiress Presumptive to The Imperial Throne of Russia, Grandduchess Maria Vladimirovna. Madrid, 1972.

LEFT: Czar Alexander II, great grandfather of the Russian claimant. Moscow, 1878. (*New York Herald Tribune*)

RIGHT: A portrait of Grand Duke Vladimir's cousin, Czar Nicholas II. Petrograd, 1911.

BELOW: Czar Nicholas, Czarina Alexandra, and their four children shortly before their assassination. Moscow, 1916. (Sovfoto)

The Spanish claimant's house in Estoril. (Finlay)

SPAIN

LEFT: His Royal Highness don Juan, Count of Barcelona. Estoril, Portugal, 1972. (Finlay) RIGHT: The most likely next King of Spain, Prince Juan-Carlos with his blind sister, Princess Marguerita. Madrid, 1967. (Brown Bros.)

LEFT: Prince Juan-Carlos with Generalissimo Franco. Madrid, 1972. RIGHT: Princess Maria del Carmen of Bourbon with baby Prince Francisco. Madrid, 1972.

BELOW LEFT: Generalissimo Franco with Prince Alphonso of Bourbon and Dampierre and Maria del Carmen. Madrid, 1972. (Oggi) MIDDLE: Franco escorts his granddaughter to her wedding. Madrid, 1972. (Oggi) RIGHT: Prince Juan-Carlos with Madame Franco, Maria del Carmen's grandmother. Madrid, 1972. (Oggi)

LEFT: His Imperial Highness Prince Osman Fuad, claimant to the throne of Turkey. London, 1969. (Monarchist League) RIGHT: King Antiochus I gazes over the mountains of Central Turkey where he ruled 100 years before Christ.

TURKEY

The Ottoman Empire reached three continents by the 14th Century. (Raphael Palacios)

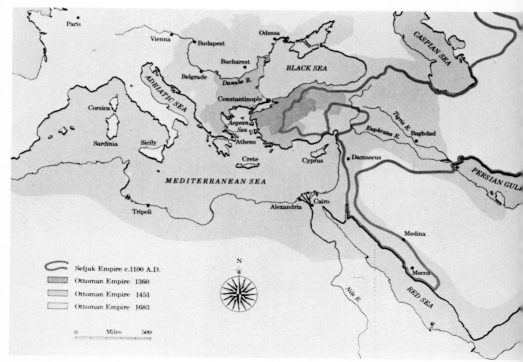

ABOVE: Prince Osman's granduncle, Sultan Abdul Hamid II, a ruthless and repressive ruler, in his carriage before being deposed by reformers. Constantinople, 1908. (Radio Times Hulton) BELOW: The ancient mystique survives in Turkish villages. Van, near the Iranian border, 1964. (Farrell Grehan)

BELOW: Colonel Mustafa Kemal, known as Ataturk— "Father Turk" — Turkey's first President. Istanbul, 1919. (Ara Güler)

BELOW: Turkish officers on the eve of World War I. Istanbul, 1915. (Ara Güler)

YUGOSLAVIA

ABOVE: Attending the christening of Crown Prince (later King) Peter of Yugoslavia. Left to right: King Alexander of Yugoslavia (father), Queen Elizabeth of Greece, baby Peter, Queen Marie of Rumania, King Ferdinand of Rumania, Duke and Duchess of York (later King George VI and Queen Elizabeth of England). Belgrade, 1923. (Culver) BELOW RIGHT: The royal exiles arrive in New York on the *S.S. Caronia*: Queen Alexandra, Crown Prince Alexander (4), and King Peter. 1949. (Brown Bros.)

BELOW: Peter and Alexandra at the Stork Club. New York, 1950. (Brown Bros.)

His Royal Highness King Peter of Yugoslavia. London, 1960.

LEFT: Queen Alexandra and King Peter of Yugoslavia visiting Sir Winston Churchill at 10 Downing Street. 1955. (Central Press) RIGHT: Queen Alexandra, King Peter, and Prince Alexander in Cortina. Italy, 1950. (Interfoto)

The wedding of King Peter and Princess Alexandra. The Duchess of Gloucester, Queen Elizabeth of England, the late King George VI, Peter, King Haakon of Norway, Prince Tomislav of Yugoslavia, Alexandra, Princess Aspasia of Greece, King George of Greece, Queen Wilhelmina of The Netherlands, Prince Bernhard of The Netherlands. London, 1944.

THE EMPIRE OF RUSSIA

His Imperial Highness Grand Duke Vladimir Cyrilovitch, Grand Duke of Russia

HOUSE OF ROMANOFF-HOLSTEIN-GOTTORP

If one were to assess the prospects of the various claimants for a return to their respective thrones, the least promising would most certainly be that of the Russian claimant, His Imperial Highness Grand Duke Vladimir Cyrilovitch, cousin of the last Czar. When the solidarity, power, and progress of Russia today are considered against the claim of one middle-aged exile, the thought may appear almost ridiculous. It is not that simple a comparison, however.

For the most cynical royalty-watcher, it can be a provocative experience to sit quietly with the present imperial family and to assess them as people, as individuals, and as a "breed." Unfortunately for them—Grand Duke Vladimir, his wife Grand Duchess Leonide, and their only child, Grand Duchess Marie—vis-à-vis the contemporary Russian mystique, there is nothing of the proletariat about them. But on the asset side, neither is there anything of the bourgeois. The vibrations are strictly royal, with subtones of intelligence, compassion, and integrity.

Vladimir dresses like a French businessman, talks like a British solicitor, and looks a bit like an American western hero. He is handsome and strong; he has a certain look in the eyes that one might guess a Romanoff could not avoid—a touch of autocracy, a suggestion of fear, and a clarity of breeding. Vladimir, a great-grandson of Queen Victoria of England, is related to virtually all the royal dynasties of Europe. He gives the impression of being capable and energetic. Leonide is an arresting beauty in the classical sense: a wonderful profile, thick dark hair, and a superb voice. She exudes an aura of peaceful but forceful authority. Her own family, which ruled Georgia for thirteen centuries and were kings of Armenia, may be the most ancient of the royal Christian dynasties. (Georgia was annexed by Imperial Russia; Leonide's brother, Prince Irakly, is the current representative of her royal house.) The breed has an indelible stamp on the Grand Duchess. Their daughter has the soft, warm eyes of her mother, and the handsome caste of her father's features. Grand Duchess Marie is healthy and strong, rippling with good humor, and blessed with great feminine attraction.

While the Russian royal family makes absolutely no concessions to the legitimacy and propriety of the Communist rule, they love Russia, are totally aware of, and proud of, her achievements, and live for the day when they can return to what they still consider their homeland.[1] It is impossible to avoid the thought that it is a tangible waste of talent and energy for Russia not to find some place in the scheme of things for this vibrant family.

Grand Duke Vladimir was born on August 30, 1917, near Borga, Finland. He is the only son and third child of Grand Duke Cyril and Grand Duchess Victoria Feodorovna, princess of Great Britain and Northern Ireland, and duchess of Saxony. When the last Czar, Nicholas II, the Czarina, four daughters, and only son and heir were assassinated by the Bolsheviks in 1918 in the foothills of the Urals, his first cousin, Grand Duke Cyril Vladimirovitch, became the head of the Imperial House. Cyril was the grandson of Alexander II, the great reformer known as the "Czar-Liberator" who emancipated the serfs during his twenty-five year reign beginning in 1855. Ironically, Alexander, the current claimant's great-grandfather was murdered by a terrorist's bomb in 1881.

The claimant's father, Cyril, an officer in the Russian Imperial Navy, died in exile in 1938, and Vladimir succeeded to the claim. The Grand Duke's full title, if he used it, would be Vladimir III, Emperor and Autocrat of All the Russias.

Vladimir went to England in 1939 where he worked in a machine factory near Peterborough. Only the manager knew who he was. Vladimir had assumed the name of Mikhailoff, the name used by Czar Peter the Great when he worked as a shipbuilder in England and Holland two centuries before. During the war Vladimir was in France until 1944, when he was deported to Germany and eventually to Austria in 1945. At one time it was falsely rumored that, during his stay in Austria, certain negotiations were initiated by Hitler, who promised a return of the Romanoffs to a puppet throne after Soviet Russia had been defeated by the German Armies; Vladimir was stalwartly opposed to Nazi policy concerning Russia. In 1946 he moved to Spain.

In 1948 in Switzerland Vladimir married Princess Leonide Bagration-Moukhransky of the royal house of Georgia, who was born in 1914 in Tiflis, the daughter of Prince George and Helen Zlotnicka. Grand Duchess Leonide was first married to Sumner Moore Kirby, who died in 1945 in a Nazi concentration camp.

Grand Duke Vladimir and the Grand Duchess have a nineteen-year-old daughter, Her Imperial Highness Grand Duchess Marie Vladimirovna, who was born in Madrid. Marie is the heiress presumptive to the imperial throne of Russia after the death of the last male member of the family. Males in the direct line have all married morganatically and their descendants, therefore, are excluded from the succession.

For this reason, and in order to forestall any unqualified claims to the succession, the Grand Duke has declared that, in the case of his demise prior to the death of the last male member of the family, Marie shall assume the rights and functions of Curator of the Throne, until she becomes head of the family, with the extinction of the male lineage.

Vladimir lives in Madrid at 13 Guisando, Cuidad de Puererta de Hierro. He is an impressive, serious man with a dignified and direct manner. He is completely fluent in Russian, English, German, French, and Spanish.

Grand Duke Vladimir is relatively well off financially, due mainly to some investments on both sides of the family and to the support of White Russian circles in various parts of the world. The claimant spends a great deal of his time communicating and corresponding with such groups. About five years ago Vladimir issued an appeal "to Russia and to the conscience of the world." He stated that the abdication of Czar Nicholas II was forced by Russian and international revolutionaries, to the eventual detriment of the Russian people by the loss of their freedom. Vladimir asserted that only freedom in Russian can assure prosperity, and that only a return to monarchy can assure freedom.

It is generally believed that the royalist (Czarist) movement in Russia itself is virtually defunct since most of the sympathizers fled by the thousands to all parts of the world. However, as ironic or even fanciful as it may seem, there are Czarists who are convinced that the movement is alive—not only among Russians in exile, but within Russia itself. There is, reputedly, an "underground" in the USSR which has nurtured a swing to monarchial sentiment in the last few years. It is said that this sentiment is particularly noticeable in the trend generally known as "Neo-Slavophil" and its underground magazine called *Veche*. Russian royalists feel that there is definite disillusionment with the present regime and its ideology, and they claim that the Russians fear the anarchy that would follow the downfall of the Soviet monolith. They have an abiding belief that the monarchy alone could provide that binding force which would prevent the Russian edifice from collapsing into chaos.

If ideologies could be swept aside for a moment, the Soviets would be the first to see true value and ability in the persons of Vladimir Cyrilovich and Leonide—Russians. But such a moment is inconceivable. Only an upheaval in the monolithic structure of the USSR would allow the Russian claimant to think seriously about his prospects. But in the turmoil and frantic eclecticism that sweeps Europe, is it too strange to believe that there is a place for the autocratic claimant in a newly autocratic Russia?

NOTES

1. Ivan Bilibin, a White Russian emigré and confidant of the imperial family who now lives in England, described the Russian monarchial position to me in 1972:

"After the defeat of the Whites in the Civil War, which followed three unconstitutional acts (the abdication of the Emperor Nicholas II for himself and his son in favor of his brother the Grand Duke Michael; the conditional abdication of the Grand Duke Michael pending the convening and decision of the Constituent Assembly which was to be organized and convened by the provisional government; and the provisional government's contravention of its terms of reference by declaring Russia a republic prior to the convention of the provisional government) the dynasty had to reassert its rightful position. In 1922, when the fate of the late imperial family was still regarded as uncertain, the Grand Duke Cyril assumed the office of Curator of the Throne. In 1924 the Grand Duke was convinced that the late imperial family and the Grand Duke Michael had been assassinated, and issued a manifesto in which he assumed the title of Emperor. An instruction was issued at the same time that he would use this title only among Russians. This drastic step was regarded as essential in order to make it clear that the acts of 1917 were null and void and that the dynasty was in no way affected by them.

"When the Grand Duke Cyril died in 1938, his son and heir, the Grand Duke Vladimir, issued a manifesto in which he stated: 'Following my father's example, in profound awareness of the sacred duty incumbent upon me, I assume by inheritance, by the supreme right of Head of the Imperial House of Russia which has devolved upon me by right of succession, all the rights and duties which belong to me by virtue of Fundamental Laws of the Russian Empire and the Statutes of the Imperial Family.' The words 'following my father's example' put it beyond all doubt that the Grand Duke assumed the title of Emperor, but he did not say so specifically, as the Grand Duke Cyril did in his manifesto of 1924. An instruction was issued at the same time from the Grand Duke's Office, stating that the Head of the Imperial House would continue to use the title of Grand Duke, thus extending to all the 'incognito' which the Grand Duke Cyril had limited to his relations with foreigners. At the same time yet another instruction was issued, stating that a number of people had sworn allegiance to the Head of the Imperial House as Emperor, and that the Grand Duke accepted their oaths.

"I think this gives a very clear picture of the Grand Duke's views in this matter. He considers that his father's assumption and use of the Imperial Title was necessary in order to secure the future of the dynasty. As this has already been done by his father, he does not consider it necessary for him to continue the use of the Imperial Title, which in conditions of exile often causes unnecessary embarrassment. The latent Imperial Title, however, implied in his accession manifesto, secures the future of the dynasty, including, for instance, the perpetuation of the grand-ducal title for future generations, which otherwise would have gone into abeyance."

THE KINGDOM OF SPAIN

1) His Royal Highness don Juan of Bourbon and Battenberg, Count of Barcelona
2) His Royal Highness don Juan-Carlos of Bourbon and Battenberg
   HOUSE OF BOURBON-ANJOU

While the prospects of the Romanoffs returning to the Russian throne are far down on the scale of chance, their Spanish cousins are happily enjoying life at the other end of the scale. The crown and throne of Spain are definitely being dusted off, and the House of Bourbon-Anjou is riding the crest of a royalist wave at the moment. (Although don Juan of Bourbon and Battenberg is the legitimate claimant and head of the house, his son Juan-Carlos has been tapped by Generalissimo Franco to be the sovereign.) The royal house of Spain will be back in business after an absence of forty years.

The historical order of antiquity of the royal houses of Europe (*see* page 217) puts Spain second after France, the most ancient. The bloodline of the Spanish royal family weaves its way in history through the kingdoms of Castile, Leon, Aragon, Navarre, Anjou, France, Naples, Prussia, Parma, the Netherlands, Austria, Bulgaria, Greece, Portugal, and England. From the eighth century to the present moment, this family has savored the sweet taste of

87

sovereignty. The Spanish claimant, His Royal Highness don Juan de Bourbon et Battenberg, count of Barcelona, reflects this history like a fine mirror.

Don Juan lives in exile in a large pleasant white house on England Road, atop a fashionable hill overlooking Estoril, Portugal. Ian Finlay, who visited don Juan in March 1972, commented on his encounter with this impressive man (*see* Interview, p. 163): "I arrived on a sunny morning and was struck by the cool, dark Iberian atmosphere within the house—the quiet, heavily draped hall, the dignified white-jacketed manservant, the African antelope heads on the walls, the magnificent, slightly faded tapestry. Don Juan's private secretary came to meet me. The secretary is an ex-Spanish Air Force Colonel, distinguished looking and dressed like an English squire in tweed jacket and cavalry twill trousers. We conversed amiably in French, and then he inquired what sort of conversation I wanted to have with don Juan—he was obviously apprehensive about any possible political context. I explained that my interest in don Juan's position was social in concept rather than political, and this seemed to dispel his fears.

"I met don Juan in his study, and received a very warm welcome. I told him that I wanted to ask him about Spain but if my questions were too pointed he must let me know. He spoke English fluently but with a heavy Spanish accent, and in a deep slow voice which matched his frame. Our discussion was most relaxed and friendly—he has a grand sense of humor and is quite outspoken. I would describe him as expansive, friendly, warm, and intelligent. He has a generous approach to things.

"When I mentioned pictures after our discussion, don Juan appeared quite nervous and rang for his secretary who proceeded first to arrange the room and then to arrange don Juan, adjusting his jacket and tie. Only then could I take pictures. And even then he was unhappy being photographed at his desk, and suggested that he would be better standing up. He was rather like a small boy who's been told how to pose in front of a camera, and was quite self-conscious about it. His shyness was very endearing in a man of his position. Don Juan was very involved in receiving people—there was someone from Madrid with him when I arrived, and someone else waiting when I left. . . ."

Don Juan was born in San Ildefonso, Spain, in June 1913. He was the third son and fifth child of King Alphonso XIII of Spain and Queen Victoria-Eugenia, Princess of Battenberg, and granddaughter of Queen Victoria of England. King Alphonso fled Spain in 1931 when he refused to abdicate after the proclamation of the Republic. Prince don Juan became the heir apparent to the rights following the renunciation of his other older brothers. When King Alphonso XIII finally abdicated his dynastic rights in 1941, don Juan became chief of the Spanish royal house, and was recognized as His Catholic Majesty, don Juan III, by the Spanish monarchists. King Alphonso was killed in an automobile accident in 1944 in Portugal; the Queen Mother died in Lausanne five years ago.

In 1935 in Rome don Juan married a cousin, the Royal Princess Maria de las Mercedes of Bourbon and Orléans, who was born in Madrid in 1910, the daughter of the crown prince of Spain, don Carlos of Bourbon, and the former Princess Louise of Orléans.

Don Juan and Princess Maria have three children: Crown Princess dona Maria of Bourbon and Bourbon (thirty-six), married to don Louis Gomez-Acebo, Viscount de la Torre, cousin of Queen Margarita of Bulgaria; Crown Prince don Juan-Carlos of Bourbon and Battenberg, Prince of Austurias (thirty-four), who is married to Her Royal Highness Sophia of Greece (thirty-four), daughter of the late King Paul of Greece and Princess Frederika, of Hanover, and sister of King Constantine of Greece; and Crown Princess Margarite (thirty-three). Crown Prince Alphonso was killed in an accident in Portugal in 1956.

Spain is most certainly the current center of all royalists' attention. The claimants have their eyes fixed on events in Madrid. Spain, under Franco, has been a monarchy without a king. The Generalissimo had made it known for years that it was his intention to restore the monarchy, and it appears that he is keeping to his word.

Before King Alphonso died in the crash, he had renounced his rights in favor of his third son, don Juan of Bourbon and Battenberg, count of Barcelona, head of the royal house. The king nominated Juan as his heir in 1935 when Juan's elder brothers renounced their rights—his son Alphonso because he married a commoner, and his son Jaime because he was a deaf-mute. Franco, however, has not been sympathetic to the relatively liberal views of don Juan, who has been in exile in Portugal.

In July 1969 Franco made the pronouncement naming as *his* successor don Juan's son, Prince Juan-Carlos, who will bear the title of prince of Spain until the moment he is called upon to take the throne restored by Franco in his name. Following Franco's speech, the Cortes (parliament) passed the Bill of Succession to the headship of state by a large majority.

Immediately after these events, don Juan issued a statement from Estoril on July 19, 1969:

In 1947, when the text of the so-called Law of Succession was made public, I expressed my reservations about and exceptions to that legal ordinance in so far as it was contrary to the historical tradition of Spain. Those warnings are seen to have been confirmed now, when after twenty years, the application of that law is announced. To carry out this operation, I have not been taken into account, nor has the freely expressed will of the Spanish people. For I am a spectator regarding decisions which may be taken in this matter and no responsibility devolves upon me in this restoration.

During the last thirty years I have frequently addressed myself to the Spanish people to put forward what I consider essential in the future

Monarchy: That the King should be King of all Spaniards, presiding over a State of justice; that the Institution should function as an instrument of national policy at the service of the people and the Crown should have power of arbitration over and outside of the groups and sectors which compose the country. And besides this, authentic popular representation; the national will represented in all organs of public life; society freely expressing its opinion through the established channels; the complete guarantee of collective and individual liberty, thus reaching the political level of Western Europe, of which Spain forms part.

This is what I wanted and desire for my people and such is the essential purpose of the monarchic Institution. I have never professed, nor do I do so now, to disunite the Spanish people. I continue to believe in the necessity of peaceful evolution from the present system towards an open course of living together democratically, the only guarantee of a stable future for our Country, which I shall continue to serve as a Spaniard and for which I desire in my heart a future of peace and prosperity.

A new wrinkle, however, was added to the situation in March 1972: The marriage of Franco's favorite granddaughter, Marie del Carmen Martinez Bordui y Franco (twenty-one), daughter of the Marquis and Marchioness of Villaverde, to His Royal Highness Prince don Alphonso of Bourbon and Dampierre (thirty-five), son of His Royal Highness don Jaime of Bourbon, duke of Anjou and Segoira—the deaf mute. Don Alphonso, don Juan's nephew, is the eldest grandson and namesake of Spain's last king, and is the current Spanish ambassador to Sweden. The sumptuous Madrid wedding of the lovely blond dona Maria del Carmen and her handsome prince had all the trappings of a royal marriage plus the possibility of dynastic intrigue.

Royalty buffs and political guessers have speculated for years that Franco would like to end his days by joining his own family to the royal line. When he chose Juan-Carlos (who was already married to Princess Sophie of Greece) as his successor, the speculation diminished. But now, the guessers have returned to the game.

The most sophisticated speculators believe that the recent alliance of Franco's family with a possible pretender means merely that Juan-Carlos will have less power than he was expected to have when he becomes king.

If the thirty-four-year-old Juan-Carlos, after Franco's departure, showed overly liberal tendencies (possibly fostered by his father) in conflict with the Franco regime's legacy, the caretakers of the autocratic government would have a ready-made royal alternative in the person of Franco's new grandson-in-law, Prince Alphonso. Alfonso and Maria made the Generalissimo a great-grandfather when Prince Francisco Alfonso Jaime Cristobal Victor was born in late November 1972—just twelve days before Franco's eightieth birthday.

But while these matters swirl, the fact remains that don Juan is dynastically the true claimant.

In October 1969 the Monarchist League in London printed the following comment in its Journal:

Immediately prior to and following the developments in July concerning the announcements by the present Head of the Spanish Government, the Chancellery was in direct touch with both His Royal Highness the Count of Barcelona and His Royal Highness Prince Juan-Carlos.

Opinion on this must be up to the individual conscience of each monarchist, but the Monarchist League, until His Royal Highness don Juan, the Count of Barcelona, has declared otherwise, consider him the Head of the Royal House of Spain and continue to be at His service and that of the Dynasty.

Don Juan has never renounced his rights—although he has come to some sort of detente with his son Juan-Carlos—and has been judicious enough to curtail his public activities in politics since 1969.

Don Juan and Princess Maria live comfortably in their "Villa Giraldo" on the outskirts of Estoril, a popular place for many years with royalty in exile. The Count of Paris, King Carol of Rumania, and others have lived in Estoril from time to time. Don Juan speaks English, French, Portuguese, German, and Italian. He is a terribly "kingly" person in the truest sense of the word. He looks as a king should look, and he acts as a good king should act. He is candid, intelligent, warm, a sportsman, a politician, a good listener and talker, ready for a laugh, and a loyal and stalwart friend to people of all walks of life. (Winston Churchill once wrote that, without doubt, the finest gentleman he had ever met was King Alphonso, don Juan's father. Reflections of this quality are seen in don Juan.)

Don Juan takes his role in life philosophically but seriously. Like the more ardent of his fellow claimants he spends a great deal of time receiving people, corresponding with sympathizers to the royalist cause, keeping in touch with politics, economics, and life in general. His office—which is administered by Colonel José A. de Lacour Macia (El Secretario Particular del Conde de Barcelona) —is busy and involved. Don Juan is financially comfortable. He may be very rich, he may be modestly well off. It is difficult to judge. He certainly is not poor. But he gives the impression of a man who could maintain his style and his love of life under any circumstances—rich or poor.

Don Juan is in the unique position of being the only claimant to the throne of a country whose government has said that it will definitely restore the monarch. The fact that politics have put his son—and possibly his nephew—in a position to receive the crown may give don Juan some uncomfortable moments. But he is a realist as well as a dynast. In the post-Franco period this may be precisely what is needed. Only time will tell—and happily for royalty-watchers, the time is distinctly foreseeable. Don Juan remains the literal claimant.

A successful return of the monarchy to Spain could have an immense impact on the prospects of many other claimants. The most constant royalty-watchers are probably the royal persons themselves. They are certainly justified in the case of Spain today.

TURKEY

His Imperial Highness Prince Osman Fuad
HOUSE OF OSMAN

The claimant to the throne of Turkey—to the sovereignty of the Ottoman Empire—takes his name from his ancestor Osman I (or "Othman" and, thereby, "Ottoman") who firmly established the dynasty of the House of Osman in the fourteenth century: Prince Osman Fuad lives today on the shores of the Mediterranean in an alien country. Less than three hundred years ago his family controlled an empire whose perimeters reached from Morocco to South Arabia, from Persia to Armenia, from Odessa to Budapest, and the lands, seas, and peoples within those boundaries. Little more than fifty years ago the last sultan of the House of Osman fled Turkey—six centuries after the dynasty had imposed its primary sway in Anatolia.

The sweep and panoply of history in Asia Minor, in what is known today as Turkey or, less familiarly, Anatolia, surprises and then boggles the minds of those whose school studies took them in books across Europe and stopped at the Bosporus. The Bible says that Noah's ark came to rest on Mount Ararat in what is now Turkey. Hittites, Phrygians, Lydians, Assyrians, Greeks, Romans, Byzantines, Mongols, Persians, and Turkomens ranged over and possessed the Anatolian lands for centuries upon centuries in a skein of crosscultures and influences. Indo-Europeans, ancestors of the Greeks, arrived in Turkey eleven centuries before Christ; Asia Minor became profoundly influenced by Hellenism.

Eventually the Seljuk Turks, originally from Persia and the Uzbek region of Russia, invaded Anatolia and dominated the vast plateau. The Turkish element grew steadily as tribes arrived in an uninterrupted flow from Central Asia and Turkestan up to the end of the thirteenth century. The word "Turkey" itself is probably derived from "T'u-chueh," the name given by the Chinese to the Western Asian ancestors of the modern Turks.

By the tenth century the Seljuk Turks had established themselves, and by the twelfth century they created the Seljuk sultanate (sultan: a king of a muslim state). The Seljuk dynasty in Asia Minor enabled the Turkish nation to control the Anatolian plateau, and ultimately to set off on the conquest of Eastern Europe—initially and very importantly the destruction of Byzantine Christian power centered in Constantinople.

In the 1300s new semi-autonomous Turkish rulers (emirs) sprang up. One was the tribe of Ogrul which had originated in the Transcaspian steppes and settled in Eastern Anatolia with the approval of the Seljuks. The Ogrul tribe of four hundred families was the origin of the Ottoman dynasty. The Ogruls (Osmanli or Ottomans) supported the Seljuks against the Mongols, and were awarded an emirate (a barony). Under the strong and ruthless leadership of successive emirs, the Ottomans assumed the sultanate from the weakened Seljuks in the latter part of the fourteenth century, and moved their goal of conquest into the Balkans.

By the sixteenth century, during the reign of Sultan Suleiman I (1520–1566) Turkey had become the leading power in Central Europe, in the Mediterranean, and in Western Europe. Turkey acted as arbiter between the major powers. The Ottoman Empire exercised its authority over Iran, Mesopotamia, Egypt, Tunisia,

Syria, Cyprus, Arabia, Iraq, Albania, Armenia, Rumania, Crete, Greece, Georgia, Hungary—and its influence throughout Europe and the Middle East. The Ottomans had extended their power even to the frontiers of Austria.

By the mid-1700's the present claimant's great-great-grandfather, Mohammed II (1785–1839), had inherited the problems and excesses of generations of super-power, riches, victories and defeats, intrigue, decadence, and eventually decline. Sultan Mohammed and his son and successor, Abdul Metid I, instituted reforms, reorganized the army, and gave the country new administrative, judicial, and financial charters.

British historian Edward Creasy says:

It is indeed a remarkable trait in the character of the first princes of the Ottoman dynasty that, unlike most conquerors, especially Asiatic ones, they did not hurry on from one war to another; but, to the contrary, they were not more eager to seize than they were cautious and earnest to consolidate. They paused over each subdued province, till, by assimilation of civil and military institutions, it was blended into the general nationality of their empire. They thus gradually molded in Asia Minor an homogenous and stable power, instead of precipitately heaping together a motley mass of ill-arranged provinces and discordant populations.

Middle Eastern expert Desmond Stewart agrees that the House of Osman had created a unique political body:

The Ottoman Empire in its prime was more like a self-perpetuating, self-enlarging corporation devoted to the promulgation of an idea, than the usual empire in which a group of outsiders dominates conquered subjects. The Ottoman state from the beginning turned those it conquered into members of its own corporate body, into its own executives. By the time of Sultan Suleiman (known as The Magnificent) the Ottomans possessed not only the best organized military force on earth—the most modern in its technology, its commissariat, and treatment of troops—but a society that was modernist and tolerant compared with those of contemporary Europe.

But the cracks in the Ottoman Empire had begun.

Although the first ten sultans were as remarkable rulers as those produced by any political system anywhere, the later sultans, with only a few exceptions, have been described by British historian Bernard Lewis as a series of "incompetents, degenerates, and misfits." Compounded autocracy and corruption grew to cancerous proportions. Royal fratricide, among other ills, became the prime vice of the Ottomans in settling questions of succession. Although fratricide was not unknown in other European royal families, the Ottomans were excessive. (As only one example, when Sultan Murad III, father of 103 children, died two hundred and fifty years ago, his heir Mohammed III murdered his nineteen surviving brothers.) Internal conflicts, rebellions among Ottoman satellites, alliance with Germany in World War I, and finally the Greek-Armenian War of Independence against Turkey (1919–1920) crushed the last strength of the Ottoman dynasty.

In 1920 a national military hero, Mustafa Kemal—later to be known as Ataturk, "father Turk"—was elected head of the new Grand National Assembly of Turkey. Three years later the Turkish Republic was proclaimed on October 29, 1923, with Kemal as its first president.

The current claimant to the Ottoman throne, His Imperial Highness Prince Osman Fuad is, to royalist supporters, *de jure* Sultan Osman IV Fuad of Turkey. Prince Osman leads a quiet single life whose principal purpose seems to be centered on preserving his ebbing energies. The Prince lives at the Martinez Hotel in Cannes on the French Riviera, but travels occasionally to Paris, London, Switzerland, and, on occasions, to Beirut and Cairo. It is impossible to assess the material comfort of the seventy-eight year old Turkish claimant. His fragile health limits any expensive activities, and it is probable that the members of the Ottoman dynasty were able to salvage a considerable fortune and to keep it in foreign banks prior to the demise of the regime in the early 1920s. Osman gives the impression of a modestly rich man savouring his twilight years.

Prince Osman Fuad was born on February 24, 1895 in Ortakoy, a suburb of Istanbul, not far from the massive castle of Rumeli Hisar built by his ancestor Sultan Mohammed II Fatih in 1452, one year before the fall of Constantinople. Osman served as a young cavalry officer with the Prussian army during the Ottoman liaison with Germany prior to and through World War I. In his twenties, he was married at Beshiktashe on the Bosporus to Lady Nabila Kerina Halim, the daughter of Their Highnesses Prince Mohammed Abbas Halim Pasha and Princess Hadidja Tevflik of Egypt. Osman and Princess Nabila Kerima were divorced in 1932; they had no children. (Nabila then married His Highness Prince Yussuf Kemal of Egypt.)

Prince Osman is the son of His Imperial Highness Mohammed Selaheddin, the eldest son of Sultan Mohammed Murad V of Turkey, and succeeded as Head of The Imperial House in 1954 when his half-brother, Prince Ahmed Nihat, died.

The Imperial House of Osman regulates its order of succession to the throne by age rather than by primogeniture. Prince Osman IV, the present claimant, therefore, is the eldest of the male descent of the Imperial Turkish House. There are twenty-four living males in direct descent: Prince Mohammed Abdul Aziz, grandson of Sultan Abdul-Aziz I (1830–1876) who was Ozman's great-grand-uncle, is second in line; the succession reaches to Orhan, twenty-third in line, who is the two year old great-grandson of Osman's late half-brother, Ahmed Nihat.

The last sultan of the House of Osman to reign in Turkey,

Mohammed VI, was sixty-five years old when he was deposed in the Autumn of 1922. Sultan Mohammed fled his palace in Istanbul and boarded a British warship for the safety of Malta. He died in exile four years later. This last of the Ottoman rulers was the current claimant's granduncle.[1]

Prince Osman, the descendant of the Conqueror of Constantinople, slowly sips his Perrier at the Martinez Hotel and thinks not of the excesses and decadence that ultimately obliterated his legacy, but of the remarkable history and accomplishment of the House of Osman. Turkey is occupied today by a population of thirty-two million people primarily Moslems of Asiatic origins. Its eyes are now turned resolutely to the West, as were the eyes of the Osmanli centuries ago. The Anatolian peninsula has seen a dozen civilizations flourish on its soil. The House of Osman held the throne for over six hundred years. Prince Osman Fuad knows it is not possible for him to see a resurgence of support for the royal position; he has reason, however, to conjecture whether the current disorder in the Middle East and the increasing militancy of Islam might not provide some eventual opportunity for the two year old Prince Orhan. The Ottomans are traditionally familiar with the remedies for turmoil. The Koran itself says: Disquiet is worse than killing.

Fifteen years ago in Paris a Turkish banker discussed the House of Osman with a reporter from the *New York Herald Tribune:* "I wonder how foolish it really is to think today of the Ottoman regime returned to power in the Middle East—or at least in Turkey? I do not mean a return of the seraglio, the harem, the veil, slaves, eunuchs, the erotic tyranny, or the privileged positions of the pashas, effendis, and beys. I mean a positive employment of the old Ottoman genius for organization and purpose. Surely some of these traits remain in the royal family blood."

NOTES

1. To offset conservative opposition to the abolition of the sultanate, the new Turkish National Assembly thought it expedient to preserve temporarily the religious functions the sultans had exercised in their role as "caliph"— i.e. successors to Mohammed; lay rulers of Islam. The deposed Mohammed VI's cousin, Prince Abdul Mejid II, a gentle scholar, was appointed caliph. Some theorists argued that this arrangement could be permanent: the president would represent secular power, and the caliph spiritual power. The argument was defeated, however, and Abdul Mejid, the current claimant's granduncle, was deposed when the caliphate was abolished in March 1924.

(A personal memoire: Prince Abdul Mejid's daughter, Princess Durru Shevkar Sultana, was for years considered by many people to be the most beautiful woman in the world. She was married to the Prince of Berar—the son of the Nizam of Hyderabad, the world's richest man—and illuminated the society pages of the newspapers in Bombay, London, and Paris. In 1950 when I was traveling by train in India from Hyderabad to Madras, my Hindu companion pointed out to me that the lady in the next compartment was the famous Princess of Berar, the daughter of the last caliph of Turkey. I contrived an encounter with her which lasted less than five minutes, and was totally dazzled by her flawless and extraordinarily exotic beauty. It will take me a lifetime to forget her face and mesmerizing charm. I am told that Princess Durru Shevkar now lives in London—a divorced and disillusioned woman in her middle fifties who still reflects the remnants of past beauty and power. Perhaps the Princess, cousin of the current Turkish claimant, symbolizes perfectly the vanished glory of the Ottomans.)

THE KINGDOM OF YUGOSLAVIA

His Royal Highness Prince Alexander
HOUSE OF KARAGEORGEVITCH

Until the early 1970s, the claimant to the Yugoslavian throne was an English soldier. It seemed to be a reasonable thing to be: He was young and single; he had no money to speak of; his father, King Peter, was only in his late forties; peacetime soldiering was not a compromising occupation, and his cousin and godmother, the queen, was the Commander in Chief of the British Armed Forces. Also, Prince Alexander's family, the Karageorgevitchs, had distinguished itself militarily in expelling the Turks from Serbia. Indeed, on the strength of that, his great-great-great-grandfather was made Prince of Serbia a hundred and fifty years ago, and his grandfather became King Alexander I of Yugoslavia.

But there were also memories and histories that dogged Alexander: His grandfather was assassinated in France, an alien army overran his country in World War II, and Britain, in the postwar period, was of no help to his father's claim to the throne. Perhaps being a soldier for England—or for any country—made no particular sense. Besides this, Alexander was an only child, and therefore, sole heir to King Peter's claim. This became increasingly pertinent when it appeared that his father, King Peter, had a major drinking problem.

King Peter was born in Belgrade in 1923, the first child of King Alexander and the Royal Princess Marie of Rumania. He succeeded to the throne upon his father's death. Peter, being only ten years old, was assisted by his pro-Axis uncle, Prince Paul, the regent. In March 1941, the Army revolted against the signing of an Axis pact, expelled Prince Paul, and placed Peter firmly on the throne at eighteen years of age. When the new government refused to honor the Yugoslavian-German treaty, Hitler's Wehrmacht invaded the country, and Peter fled with his government to England where he continued to hope and struggle for the crown.

In November 1945 the one-party Yugoslav Constituent Assembly proclaimed Yugoslavia a National Federal Popular Republic. King Peter refused to accept the decision, but the United States and Great Britain recognized the new republic.

A great-great-grandson of Queen Victoria, King Peter was a slender man with straight black hair, a prominent nose, sad eyes, and an excellent sense of humor. He was married in London in 1944 to another great-great-grandchild of Victoria, Her Royal Highness Princess Alexandra of Greece, daughter of King Alexander I and the former Princess Aspasia of Greece. When she was sixteen years old, Alexandra had politely declined a formal marriage proposal by King Zog of Albania. Peter and the lovely Alexandra lived a nomadic and eventually sorrowful life in London, Surrey, Paris, Cannes, New York, Monte Carlo, and Madrid. Their marriage had been a love-match, and Prince Alexander's birth in London in 1945 capped their happiness in the face of heavy political uncertainties and the beginnings of a financial drain. When they could not afford Claridges Hotel in London, they moved to a flat in the Yugoslav Embassy-in-Exile on Upper Grosvenor Street.

Peter, Alexandra, and Prince Alexander moved to New York in 1948, where the king found work as a consultant on international political matters. They lived in the Carlyle Hotel, then in an apartment on East Fifty-seventh Street near the East River; by 1949

Peter's political and financial speculations had left them hopeless and penniless. Alexander, who lived in a separate apartment with his nannie, was left in school in New York while his parents returned to Europe to seek some support. The young prince later lived with his grandmother, Queen Aspasia of Greece, in Venice, and went to school in Switzerland. King Peter and Queen Alexandra found no solutions to their sorrows.

After marital problems sparked by woes on all sides, dwindling health, and years of frustration, King Peter died, practically destitute, in California in 1971 at the age of forty-seven. Prince Alexander became head of the house of Karageorgevitch upon his father's death, and is known to Yugoslav Monarchists as King Alexander II.

King Peter's demise was sad. In 1971 he was living as a guest in the house of a friend, Dr. Louis Scarrone, on East Sixty-fourth Street in New York City. Queen Alexandra had gone to her mother's villa in Venice. Peter was nervous, depressed, and dependent upon drink to raise his spirits. He tried to find a job as a European representative of an American firm, but his failing health and lack of confidence undermined his efforts. Dr. Scarrone prevailed upon the king to undergo treatment in Mt. Sinai Hospital, New York. Peter left the hospital, and after disappearing for a week, was found in the Delmonico Hotel, and returned to Scarrone's house.

King Peter then went to California at the invitation of an ardent American lady royalty-watcher. The parties and the drink crushed the last spark of this gentle exile, and he died of acute alcoholism in Los Angeles on November 3 of that year. King Peter's funeral was held at the monastery of the Serbian Church in Libertyville, Illinois, and memorial services were held in England and Greece, attended by representatives of virtually all the European royal houses.

Crown Prince Alexander has not officially taken the title of king.

He has made no public statements, and has maintained a very low profile. This is not because Alexander is, by nature, shy or uninterested in Yugoslavia; it is principally because he had been serving a tour of duty in a British cavalry unit in Germany. As a member of Her *British* Majesty's forces it would not have been appropriate for him to make dynastic noises while in uniform.

Royalty-watchers can deduce, however, that the old family pressures may be still at work in spite of Alexander's silence: His engagement to Her Imperial and Royal Highness Princess Dona Maria da Gloria of Orléans and Braganza was announced on December 21, 1971. Princess Maria da Gloria is the elder daughter of His Imperial and Royal Highness Prince dom Pedro of Orléans and Braganza (first cousin of the head of the imperial house of Brazil) and of Her Royal Highness Princess dona Maria de la Esperanza of Bourbon of Orléans and Braganza (half-sister of His Royal Highness the late don Alfonso of Bourbon, crown prince of Spain). Prince Pedro is the brother of the Countess of Paris, wife of the French claimant. Alexander and Dona Maria da Gloria were married in the summer of 1972, and now live in Petropolis, Brazil, where Alexander is in the investment business.

There is some evidence that a degree of sentiment for the house of Karageorgevitch remains in Yugoslavia. The present Tito regime, however, has strongly suppressed any public expression of this sentiment. King Peter believed that he was betrayed—or at least made expendable—by the diplomatic moves of Churchill and Roosevelt after World War II, and that one day he would be recalled by his people. There are indications that a monarchist underground movement exists today in Yugoslavia, but it is difficult to measure its degree.

Yugoslav politics are volatile and unpredictable. In early 1972 there was a wave of separatist unrest among the Croatians, followed by a purge of Croat "Nationalists." The separatist movement may be serious enough to cause civil strife. If the eighty-year-old Tito is not strong enough to hold the federal structure together, anything might happen.

In the tongues of Serbo-Croatian, Slovenian, Macedonian, and Albanian, in the churches and mosques of Eastern orthodoxy, Roman Catholicism, and Islam, and in the towns and villages spread over ninety-nine thousand square miles, there are voices debating the proper course for this country of twenty million people. The syndrome of Balkan political volatility may again be at work.

The current Yugoslav claimant is a close cousin of the present sovereigns of Belgium, Denmark, England, Norway, Sweden, and Greece, and of the Duke of Edinburgh, Crown Princess Sophia of Spain and Greece, Juan-Carlos of Spain, the Italian Duke of Aosta, and Crown Prince Louis-Ferdinand of Prussia. His maternal grandmother's family, the Phanariotes, trace their descent from the Greek Byzantine emperors. Prince Alexander came through the crucible of his terrible childhood a strong, cautious man who has earned the sympathy and possibly the support of many of his royal kinsmen. In 1956 his mother, Queen Alexandra, recalled when, as exiles, she and King Peter took year-old Prince Alexander to call on his great-great-aunt, Queen Mary of England, in Marlborough House ten years before. Queen Mary said to Peter: "It may not be easy, but you must never forget you are a king!" Perhaps Alexander allows this thought to spin from time to time.

Three years ago the memoirs of Prince George Karageorgevitch, who lives in Belgrade, were serialized in a Yugoslav newspaper, the circulation of which is reported to have soared. (*Memoari*, Jugoslovenska Kujiga Terazija, Belgrade, $5.) Turmoil in Yugoslavia could ignite a traditionalist fervor and make the people yearn for something more tangible than memoirs. If so, there could be a young Slavic prince and his royal bride ready to accept the call. Alexander would come with very sound credentials.

PART THREE

Daylight and Magic

I wonder if it is not a mistake to consider these claimants as merely the dross of forgotten epoques, regal dinosaurs extinct among the living. Could not their abilities and heritage, dedication and intelligence be put to use? Why is an updated monarchy more out of the question than a self-perpetuating dictatorship or a democracy whose government changes violently every decade or less? The concept of a reasonable, intelligent, and dedicated sovereign cannot possibly be more bizarre than the fact of a General Amin, a Doctor DuValier, a Mussolini, or a Hitler.

Monarchy has been criticized for the cost of its maintenance. In a sense this is a valid criticism, but no more valid than objections to the cost of almost any kind of government, and less valid when compared to others. Monarchy can be big business. The queen of England employs nine hundred people, including a domestic staff of two hundred that runs her five residences. But the British Civil List (her "allowance" from the government) is only $1.14 million per year.

This cannot even compare to the cost of operating the exemplary democracy of the world—the United States of America. Setting aside the astronomical cost of *running* the American republic, the 1972 *election* campaign costs alone topped $400 million. *The New York Times* on November 19, 1972, reported that: ". . . By all estimates, when the final official campaign contribution and expenditure figures are computed, the recent election at all levels will prove to have been roughly a $400 million enterprise. . . ." The presidential campaign cost about $100 million, senate and congressional campaigns $100 million, gubernatorial and state legislature contests $100 million, and local elections $100 million. The all-time nonpresidential high in campaign spending was Nelson Rockefeller: He spent $7.7 million in winning reelection as governor of New York State in 1970. Sums of money like this put to shame even the most opulent potentates of history. Louis XIV and some of the Romanoffs would have been hard put to spend amounts like these for promotional purposes.

Kings could conceivably be put back on thrones without the trappings but with "salaries" (Civil Lists) equal to the going rate for the job of monarch. Giving Queen Elizabeth a hypothetical raise to $2 million annually for a job well done and using that as a base, and computing the other claimants' possible "salaries" relative to their populations and in direct ratio to the population of Great Britain and its possessions (135 million people), the total annual cost in compensation for the twelve currently kingless European thrones would be $7 million—about 2 percent of the total money spent in the last United States election campaign.

The yearly stipends for the reestablished monarchs, on the above basis, would be: King Leka of Albania (population 1.6 million), $24,000; Archduke Otto of Habsburg (population 17 million—combined Austria/Hungary), $250,000; the Count of Paris or Prince Louis Napoleon (population 46 million including French possessions), $680,000; King Simeon of Bulgaria (population 7.8 million), $115,000; King Umberto of Italy (population 49.4 million), $710,000; Crown Prince Louis-Ferdinand (population 72 million—combined East/West Germany), $1.06 million; the O'Conor don, Lord Inchiquin, or Lord O'Neill (population 4.3 million—combined Northern Ireland/Republic of Ireland), $63,-000; dom Duarte of Portugal (population 23 million including

LEFT: H.R.H. Prince Robert of Bourbon-Parma. 1960. RIGHT: H.R.H. Prince Albert of Bavaria. 1967. (H. List)

OTHER CROWNS AND OTHER CLAIMANTS

RIGHT: H.R.H. Prince Renier of The Two Sicilies, 1967. (Donnert)

LEFT: T.R.H. Prince Ernest-August and Princess Ortrud of Hanover. 1967. (Presse Seger)

RIGHT: T.R.H. Prince Frederick-Christian of Saxony and Princess Elizabeth-Helen of Thurn and Taxis. 1967.

BELOW LEFT: T.R.H. Duke Philip and Duchess Helen of Wurtemberg. 1966. (Presse Seger)

LEFT: H.M. King Boudouin I of Belgium. (Reporters Associes) RIGHT: H.M. Queen Margrethe of Denmark.

PRESENT ROYAL AND REIGNING FAMILIES

LEFT: King Constantine II of Greece. Deposed, June 1973. RIGHT: H.M. Queen Elizabeth II of England. (United Press)

ABOVE LEFT: H.S.H. Prince Franz-Josef II of Liechtenstein. (Camera Press)

RIGHT: H.R.H. Grand Duke Jean of Luxemburg. (Edouard Kutter)

LEFT: H.S.H. Prince Rainier III of Monaco.

ABOVE LEFT: H.M. Queen Juliana of The Netherlands. (Max Koot)

ABOVE RIGHT: H.M. King Carl XVI Gustaf of Sweden. (Bergem)

RIGHT: H.M. King Olaf V of Norway.

MAPS

Europe about 1360.

Europe in 1721.

ABOVE: Europe in 1815 (after Treaty of Vienna). BELOW: Europe in 1914.

possessions), $340,000; King Michael of Rumania (population 18.4 million), $270,000; Archduke Vladimir of Russia (population 213 million, USSR), $3.15 million; the Count of Barcelona or Prince Juan Carlos of Spain (population 30.3 million including possessions), $450,000; Prince Osman Fuad of Turkey (population 32 million), $480,000; and Prince Alexander of Yugoslavia (population 19 million), $280,000. King Constantine of Greece (population 8.5 million) $123,000.

There is not one of the claimants who would not snap at the terms; in fact, most of them—with Olympian rectitude—would accept meager compensation for the opportunity to reestablish their line and to serve their country.

Somerset Maugham said that we all, in varying degrees, possess a "faculty for myth." Underneath it all, we love grandeur and mystery. Perhaps it is the protest of romance against the commonplace of life, Maugham felt. And sometimes, particularly in these days of grinding realities, the protest is essential for survival. A role for the claimants in the modern world could provide an ingredient long absent from Western politics.

This is not to say: Forget the circumstances, bring back the pomp! Any reestablished positions for the crownless royal houses should have some clout—well proscribed to be sure. Rollo May, an American moralist and psychoanalyst, sees an important relationship between Power and Innocence. To Lord Acton's famous maxim—power tends to corrupt and absolute power corrupts absolutely—May counters: Weakness tends to corrupt and impotence corrupts absolutely. He says that violence arises not from too much power but from too little. Power without love leads to manipulation, he feels, but love without power is just sentimentality. The claimants require more than sentimentality to be viable.

Politics and politicians are awash with creativity and imagination, coupled with a desperate sense of the practical. Surely there exist, on the European scene, political minds that could employ the talents and charismas of the jobless royals. There must be a means to utilize the assets without tarnishing the magic. A fragile package, particularly if mixed with a dash of practicality and just a bit of power.

There may be some danger in stripping the mystery from monarchy. A hundred years ago British social scientist Walter Bagehot wrote: "Above all our royalty is to be reverenced. In its mystery is its life; we must not let daylight in upon magic." But the English seem to have found the way. A Harris Poll conducted in 1971 showed that most Britons believe that the monarchy not only acts as a check against military or political leaders becoming too powerful, but also sets standards of morality and family behavior. (The poll also indicated that, if a vote were held, Elizabeth would overwhelmingly be elected queen.) The pragmatic British do not seem to mind little touches of anachronistic splendor amid the workings of government: in the day-to-day mechanics of the Commonwealth it matters not that each morning, while the queen eats breakfast, a bagpiper plays outside her window, or that her butterpats carry the royal monogram. The magic is there and so is the sovereign. The government functions.

Wouldn't it be worthwhile at least to crank the monarchial approach into Europe's bulging bag of government alternatives? There are sovereign states that are socialist, communist, fascist, and republican. There are combinations. There are also the nine hereditary monarchies still alive (and mostly well) in Europe. Why shouldn't the ousted sovereigns, the claimants, be given some political consideration? They are waiting, and most are ready. It may be time for the sun to shine on these sovereigns in the shadows, these monarchs-in-waiting.

Whether or not the shadows remain, the kings without thrones will continue the vigil over their claims, as will their heirs for generations to come. The game of royalty-watching has a distinct future. So may the claimants.

Interviews

An interview with any claimant is—to the average royalty-watcher—a tantalizing experience. The impact, of course, differs with the personalities of the claimants themselves, the ages of their houses, the current circumstances in which they live, the prospects for their return to a position of importance, and to many other factors that would be involved in any human equation. Geography, however, may have played a very important role in sculpting generic differences in the claimants' attitudes toward their own positions.

For example, it is probably true that monarchial feelings are more ingrained and vibrant in the "southern" parts of Europe than in the "northern." Traditionalism dies harder in southern places. One can draw his own conclusions regarding *why*. On the other hand, the northern European monarchies—notably the Scandinavian kingdoms—are alive and well. England can be, in this sense, considered a northern type. Possibly southern places are more traditional but more emotional, more apt to be swayed and to be changed. Climate and geography, most likely, play parts in the monarchial scheme of things, as they certainly do in all others.

There follow casual but serious verbatim interviews with four claimants: Two are of one "type" and two are of another. The arbitrary distinction is between the GERMANIC types in contrast to the LATIN types: Otto von Habsburg and Louis-Ferdinand von Hohenzollern, and don Juan of Spain, and dom Duarte of Portugal. This is a whimsical choice of differences, but one type (Otto and Louis-Ferdinand) can be considered "European"; the other type (don Juan and dom Duarte) can be looked upon as "Iberian." Geography made the difference.

For centuries upon centuries the Pyrenees have kept the Iberian Peninsula a place unto itself. The people, attitudes, cultures, and mentalities of the Iberians—today known too broadly as the Spanish, the Portuguese (and, indeed, the Basques)—have been distinctive and special. Of course there was contact with the countries across the Pyrenees to the north, and with others to the south, west, and east. But, in any direction, the Iberians have had to cross natural obstacles like mountains, oceans, and seas to do so. While Iberia has not been hermetically sealed, it has been at least isolated enough to develop a pristinely distinct people. Many of these characteristics remain today.

There is even a distinct and apparent difference between the current Iberian claimants and those across the Pyrenees. The non-Iberian claimants—i.e. all claimants except don Juan of Spain and dom Duarte of Portugal—are from countries that make up the major body of Europe where there are some natural obstacles (mountains, rivers, plains) but none as uniquely isolated by topography and geography as the Spanish and the Portuguese.

There is a further subdistinction in these interviews which can be noted: One "European" claimant is a political pragmatist (Otto von Habsburg), and the other a fatalist (Louis-Ferdinand); one "Iberian" claimant is a realist (don Juan), and the other is a passivist (dom Duarte). All four combine common elements. All are different, all are gentlemen in the truest sense of the word, and all, fundamentally, are traditionalists. All are persons to be listened to. It is also to be remembered that, in spite of topography and geography, these four houses are ultimately and closely related.

The following discussions took place in the winter of 1972.

1) INTERVIEW WITH OTTO VON HABSBURG
February 1972

QUESTION: At the moment, you are a private citizen living in Germany?

Otto von Habsburg: Yes. But I'm more in Austria than in Germany. I was not permitted to return to Austria until the year 1967. So this was why I was established in Germany since the year 1954. And consequently with my children, who were only permitted to return to Austria in 1969; some of them are to the point in school where I couldn't very well take them to the Austrian schools because they are ending their studies now.

Q.:   They're at school in Germany?

O.v.H.:   Yes, that's why I still maintain this residence. But I am much more in Austria than I am in Germany now.

Q.:   I understand that you're becoming more and more active in Austria—for instance, in March will you be directing youth seminars there, and speaking extensively? Will your ambition in the future perhaps be to live again in Austria?

O.v.H.:   Certainly, certainly yes. But I am just looking now for a place—I know already approximately where I shall be, near Innsbruck, in Tyrol.

Q.:   You have been living in Pocking for some time. Did you choose to live there because it was close to Austria?

O.v.H.:   Yes, exactly, because it was the most convenient place close to Austria which could be found at the time when I came here in '54.

Q.:   Do you perhaps also feel that Bavaria is more like Austria and more sympathetic to it in temperament?

O.v.H.:   Well, of course there is a *lot* of solidarity between Bavaria and Austria. But at the time it was only a choice of convenience. And then my wife had lived here in the area for a long time before we got married in '51—so she liked it.

Q.:   As you say, you are living as a private citizen here. To what extent are you allowed to be quite private in your life, and to what extent do your, if you like, hereditary obligations still affect you in day-to-day life?

O.v.H.:   Well, I am pretty free in doing whatever I want, you see—I am not very tied down by obligations, you know, let us say hereditary obligations—you are thinking namely, I think, of ceremonial sorts of obligations.

Q.:   Absolutely. Are there any, so to speak, *royal* duties which you still discharge?

O.v.H.:   No. None at all. You see . . . I had to make a choice, you see; you either take on a certain amount of pageantry or else you go and engage yourself in politics direct—or, if you want, some other people might engage themselves in business. You see, life is too short to do the two things at the same time. So I practically canceled out all social life—that sort of side of life.

Q.:   At the ceremonial level.

O.v.H.:   Ceremonial and social. I practically never go out for dinners. I never go out for any sort of festivities.

Q.:   Really!

O.v.H.:   Yes. I have not the time. For instance, let's take this

year; from now until New Year, with the exception
of the month of August, there is not *one* Saturday or
Sunday when I don't have already my political engagements—meetings and so on. So that takes care of
all my needs to do something in the evening.

Q.:   May I take you up on a point there. When you speak
of *political* engagements or political involvement one
almost inevitably thinks in terms of party politics on
some level. But I gather from all your writings that
your political concern is largely supranational rather
than national.

O.v.H.:   Yes, exactly. I am vice-president of the Pan-European
movement. We have organizations in Austria—the so-
called Aktion-Osterreich-Europa, for the great mass,
the Pan-European movement, which is more for the
intellectuals, and the Neu-Europaische-Generation,
which is for the young. These are working in public
opinion toward the goal of European unification—
primarily to make Austria conscious of this, and to
bring about or to force the Austrian government to
act in the sense which we think right, namely, to bring
Austria as far as possible toward European unification
and to take initiatives even beyond the others, if possible.

Q.:   Do you feel that Austria, in terms of European movements, is slightly more insular than other countries?

O.v.H.:   I will tell you—yes—by its development, of course. First
of all the four-power occupation had led Austria into
an insular development before the foreign occupation
ceased in 1956. That is to say that in the exciting
times of Robert Schumann, Austria had to stay aloof
by necessity. Then secondly of course we have the state
treaty and the neutrality status, which is creating some
problems. I don't think it's decisive. I think we can
do things regardless of it. But it is an easy pretext for

doing nothing. We have tried in Austria a technique which is rather different from those of other countries. The European movement in Austria is very much down in the streets. It's not as it would be in France or in Germany, on a rather high level.

Q.:   Yes, in France it's always been rather a matter for political *idealists*—like Schumann.

O.v.H.:   Exactly, and then you don't go down into the streets in France. We do. We do a great deal of that.

Q.:   That leads me on to another point about which I wanted to ask you. You mention the streets. Since 1919, the one *significant* call for your return to Austria was in fact on the part of the Christian Syndicates.

O.v.H.:   Yes, but that was before 1938.

Q.:   This was effectively the Workers' party, was it not?

O.v.H.:   Yes, it was the Christlich Soziale Partei.

Q.:   This obviously came as a totally spontaneous move on their part. What was *your* reaction when they called for your return?

O.v.H.:   Well, I was of course very much ready to cooperate on any of these things. It was the time of the fight against Hitler. It was an entirely different condition than it is today, because at that time the broader idea of a European unity, while it existed on paper, was not yet that lively reality it is today. So it was mostly the problem of keeping that country out of the grip of Hitler. Few then realized already what Hitler was; at that time we still had the Chamberlains and what-nots in the world who had illusions about him.

Q.:   This was about 1936.

O.v.H.:   That really started in 1933. And then went on crescendo until 1938, after which, you know, Austria was occupied by the Germans.

Q.:   Mentioning the Anschluss and occupation, I believe
              that at one stage Hitler approached you, is this not so?

O.v.H.:   Yes, but that was back in 1932. This was the very first
              time of his getting close to power. I was at that time
              in Berlin working at the Agrarian Institute of the
              Berlin University of Agricultural and Social Sciences
              and I was approached first by Prinz August Wilhelm
              von Hohenzollern, who was one of the sons of the
              former German emperor, Wilhelm II, and who was
              an outright roaring Nazi—he was a member of parlia-
              ment for the Hitler party. He tried to make a rendez-
              vous between Goering and myself. That I had no
              major objection to—I wasn't particularly interested,
              but I had no major objection. But then it came out
              that Hitler wanted to be at the rendezvous too. And
              he at that time, thinking already in terms of bringing
              Austria into the fold, just as he had used the Hohen-
              zollerns to promote his cause in Germany, wanted me
              to promote his cause in Austria. That is to say, to get
              the traditionalist element of the country to join his
              side. That, of course, I would never have been willing
              to do. So I never went to that rendezvous with Goer-
              ing—I turned it down.

Q.:   Then after the Anschluss you moved to America.

O.v.H.:   No—only after the fall of Paris. I was in Europe most
              of the time of the Phoney War. I went to America for
              the first time in my life during the Phoney War in
              the winter of 1939/40 at the invitation of President
              Roosevelt. Then I returned to Europe. Then came the
              end of France and after that I was in America until
              1944.

Q.:   How did you find reaction to you in America where
              monarchy is utterly novel?

O.v.H.:   I, of course, wasn't promoting very much of the mon-
              archy idea at the time. You see, my main subject was

the reestablishment of Austrian independence. I wasn't working for monarchy then because I very much feel that all problems of domestic affairs have to be discussed only on the national ground, and cannot be discussed abroad.

Q.: At the end of the war, when you returned to Austria, the *then* occupying Soviets . . .

O.v.H.: Yes, kicked me out.

Q.: Kicked you out, to put it politely. There was also I think a suggestion that later in the 1940s the Soviets themselves made an approach to you.

O.v.H.: No. That's not true.

Q.: It has been said.

O.v.H.: It has been said, but it's not true.

Q.: The question of the Soviets and of the *East* brings me to ask you about Hungary, and your feelings and affections for Hungary, because everyone thinks of you now solely in terms of Austria, but until 1919 one thought simultaneously of Austria and Hungary.

O.v.H.: Yes, exactly. Well, I, of course, feel very strong ties to Hungary—I speak Hungarian as well as I speak German, and I still maintain contacts with some of the Hungarians who live abroad. But right now politically the only thing one can do in the West [of Europe] for Hungary is to see to it that the West be united as fast as possible—that we have the United States of Europe here, in order to give all those nations, who are now separated from Europe, an alternative when the time comes—God knows when it's going to come, but it will come one day.

Q.: You speak consistently in terms of a united Europe. Do you not feel that the actual concept of a united

Europe is almost contradictory to the concept of national monarchies?

O.v.H.:   Yes, it is—to a *certain* extent—it is not wholly contradictory, because after all, a united Europe would still preserve certain individualities. I don't think that a united Europe would ever be a copy, say, of the Soviet Union or of China or of the United States of America. We have always been more diverse, and I think to a certain extent our diversity has been one of our wealths. I still can conceive that a united Europe would be made up of monarchies as well as of republics. But let us say the united Europe, as such, certainly is not to be identified with excessive national sovereignty, because that would be dangerous.

Q.:   On the point of the possibility of monarchy within a united Europe, how do you rate the prospects of other European claimants?

O.v.H.:   Well, first of all, I am not a claimant to the throne— you see, I want to make that very clear. Let us say I represent a certain tradition, of course, and I'll keep up that tradition. But I think that this tradition must be adapted to changing times. Consequently say, in the sense of a claimant, I am not a claimant to the throne of Austria. You see, it is very hard to assess exactly the possibilities or the nonpossibilities. I would say the only one who really will certainly get to the throne is Juan-Carlos in Spain. He has been extremely able in putting his cause into the line of general developments of the country; so that he will be a sort of continuity, as all life of a nation is a continuity. Then of course the Spanish monarchy fell much later. You see legitimacy is something so terribly intangible that it never survives the generation which has seen its end.

Q.:   You think not?

O.v.H.:   No.

Q.:   And yet the legitimists in Austria still regard you as Emperor Otto I.

O.v.H.:   Practically, no, no. I have tried to reeducate them as much as I could on that subject.

Q.:   Do you ever find yourself addressed as Emperor Otto?

O.v.H.:   Well, it happens still with some quite old people. When I see that I can do it in a charitable way, I ask them not to use any titles. If it is not possible, well, I just leave them as they are, but generally I try. People who work with me never use any titles.

Q.:   Do you refer to yourself as Doktor von Habsburg?

O.v.H.:   Not even "von"—Doktor Habsburg. This is considered according to the Austrian law.

Q.:   Has a funny situation ever arisen on people discovering who you are—I mean you appear as a totally private citizen and people suddenly discover . . .

O.v.H.:   It's impossible in Austria—*almost* everybody knows me. From recognition. The people have an extraordinary memory for faces—television aiding, and papers aiding.

Q.:   Has it happened elsewhere that you've been suddenly discovered by people who didn't in fact know who in fact you were?

O.v.H.:   Well, you see, in Europe I am generally quite broadly known. I can't easily pass without being recognized.

Q.:   Do you find this ever a great hindrance?

O.v.H.:   Well, sometimes it's a hindrance, but once you are accustomed to live with it . . .

Q.:   Can I ask you some questions about the past, reaching back possibly as far you you remember? In 1919 you went into exile with your father. I believe that then you would have been perhaps seven years old.

O.v.H.:   Yes, I was. I was born in 1912.

Q.:   Does your memory reach to then?

O.v.H.:   Oh, sure, sure. It reaches even further back—I remember the funeral of Emperor Franz Joseph. You know these big events naturally are deeply engraved in the memory—I remember the coronation of my father, I remember the revolution, I remember certain of the major battles of World War I—so you see you just sort of lived into these matters.

Q.:   Well, in 1919 you went into exile with your father. He came back to Hungary in 1921.

O.v.H.:   Yes, twice in 1921. And then we went to Madeira.

Q.:   And you were with him in Funchal.

O.v.H.:   Yes, but you see, we, the children, arrived in January and he died already on the first of April. It will be fifty years this year.

Q.:   I suspect, if I may ask you, that even at his death he still was very unreconciled to the idea of the collapse of the empire.

O.v.H.:   Well, he felt that . . . I wouldn't say that he was unreconciled, if you consider this as a, let us say, an unhappy man. But he was determined to carry on. That's certain.

Q.:   And did he impress on you any strong request to carry on yourself—obviously he did.

O.v.H.:   Well, it was obvious—he never had to impress it particularly, you see. It was just there.

Q.:   I'm going to ask you something again about the 1966 decision which allowed you to return to Austria. When it is read in black and white it appears as if it was a popular ban to keep you from the country, which lasted until 1966. But in fact it did not at all reflect popular opinion.

O.v.H.: No. It is very hard to say what exactly popular opinion is. I am not Dr. George Gallup and consequently I don't know exactly how the percentages stood. But it was always a razor-thin affair between a certain type of leadership of the Socialist party, which is now no more in public office and—as you know—in Austria we have three parties in the parliament: we have the People's party, which is often referred to as a conservative party—it is much broader than that—you know you can explain the People's party only in an American context. It's like the Republican and the Democratic parties—like a Noah's Ark in which a lot of things are. Then we have the Liberal party, the Freiheitliche Partei Osterreichs, which is a very small party, and which has been rather fickle in its political line—it's not very clearly circumscribed. At the time when I had the main difficulties it was because the Socialists had made an arrangement with the Liberal party for this resolution against me which obtained a majority in the House and did not obtain a majority in the Senate. Later on at the trial of the former head of the trade unions, Mr. Ollar, it came out that they had paid in hard cash for the vote of the Liberal party. So that it was more of a parliamentary maneuvering then anything. Afterwards when I had been able to return, it clearly proved that this was no great issue for the people as such. They were interested, of course, because it was debated everywhere. . . .

Q.: Did you take advantage of the decision immediately?

O.v.H.: No, not immediately—it took me a few weeks to take advantage of it, because I wanted to have things simmer down—I didn't know the country at the time quite well—I knew only indirectly. And so I didn't want to raise any sort of real rumpus about the matter, so I used the progressive tactics and I think they proved quite effective because there were never any major incidents—there were some little storms but nothing of importance.

Q.: And since 1966 you've returned constantly, and perhaps ever-increasingly.

O.v.H.: Yes. I started out at the end of 1967 to speak at public functions—first at smaller ones, then at larger ones and so on.

Q.: When you say public functions, at what sort of level did these functions take place?

O.v.H.: Oh, all sorts. The first speech I made in Austria was at the student organization for the University of Innsbruck. The second—I don't even remember what it was—I think in Linz, also for students, and then it continued that way. Now it's all sorts of things. Let's take the last weekend; on Friday evening I was speaking to a big meeting of the old Innviertel—the westernmost part of Upper Austria—where the farmers' organization Maschinenring had its annual general assembly. I spoke there on Friday night. Then on Saturday night I spoke at a completely public meeting also in Upper Austria. And in the afternoon I had had a discussion with students near Ried-in-Innkreis and then on Sunday night I spoke—that was a smaller meeting of the European Documentation Center, which is a meeting more of intellectuals and industrialists and business people. Well, these are the sorts of things—it's a great variety.

Q.: You constantly mention students. Do you have a particular concern for youth—I notice that next month you are to direct two youth seminars.

O.v.H.: Well, I would say, it's very much mutual. It is developing very fast. I get a great many invitations from such student groups—I do quite a bit with them. I do quite a bit with the last years in what in America would be called colleges, because that is when I think they can be best trained for political action later on. So we have these seminars—which were developed by the young themselves, you see—they invented the idea and it's sort of snowballing.

Q.: Talking about the young, can I move on to a more personal aspect. You have five daughters . . .

O.v.H.: Yes. Five daughters and two sons.

Q.: How do you feel that being the children of Otto von Habsburg affects them at the moment?

O.v.H.: Well, I don't think it affects them particularly, except that of course they are in a very strongly political atmosphere, and seem to take naturally to it.

Q.: Including even the girls?

O.v.H.: Well, it all depends—some of them do and some of them don't. But three of the five do very definitely. You see, for instance, my eldest daughter, who is now eighteen, has already taken my place on several occasions where I just couldn't—I just hadn't the time to be in three places at the same time.

Q.: And this is again on a political level?

O.v.H.: Purely, yes. I send her only to young groups for the time being—people of her own age or a little bit older.

Q.: Can I ask you something also quite personal. Your father was an extremely religious man—his atmosphere of extremely fervent Catholicism is very celebrated. Presumably you were brought up in this atmosphere.

O.v.H.: Exactly.

Q.:   How do you feel it fits in, in the young world of today especially which has changed so much since your
father's time?

O.v.H.:   I wouldn't say it has . . . let us say it has changed outwardly very much; inwardly not. You see, the forms of
certain religious practices have certainly changed con-
siderably, say in the last thirty or forty years, but the
inward need of religion still remains very strong. And
the attitude toward religion is, I think, much the
same as it was before, though it has some different
emphases.

Q.:   One of your books is called *A Politics for the Year
2000*. Do you think that a political scheme for that
time must take monarchy, the monarchial concept in
Europe, into account at all?

O.v.H.:   Well, I will tell you. One has first to define what monarchy is, *really*. You see monarchy is—if you go to the
fundamentals and now get rid of the trappings—the
twin notion that we need a mixed form of state where
not all the sources of sovereignty are the same. Because once you have just *one* source of sovereignty,
there is a great deal of danger that this one source may
become easily totalitarian. As you know, in our times
the danger of totalitarianism, I think, is much more
alive, though not so outwardly visible, than it was say
twenty or thirty years ago. The decisive phenomena
of the last ten years is that power has lost its natural
limits. You see, up to, say, 1960, each power, whether
in international life or in national life, had its limitations in nature itself—the tyrant was limited by the
extent to which he could send his aircraft and send
his motorized troops. And domestically there was still
what we might call the zone of privacy. Now these
two have ceased to exist in the last ten years. Through
the ICBMs a tyrant can today threaten all nations at

the same time—or as Louis Armand had put it, the great event of our days is that each person at any time and in every place of the world can be seen and killed. And that is a fact, you know—it's the fundamental fact. And the second fact is that within the country you have exactly the same thing today. The all-seeing eye is already a reality; the Vietnam war, for instance, has developed photographic equipment that can photograph across walls in total darkness. In other words, even the privacy of the catacombs has ceased to exist—plus the fact that the brainwashing techniques, as we have seen in China, practically permit today manipulation of any sort of crowd under almost all circumstances. A government which has no longer any sort of moral limitations, which does not acknowledge any sort of moral code, is almost almighty in relation to its citizens. And that of course means that we must, in all our political organizations, think primarily in terms of how to defend ourselves against this unlimited power within the country. And the second element which monarchy represents, say as an outward phenomenon of something which is much deeper, is the idea of continuity in the direction of the country. Now for instance I would say that many of the features of France's Fifth Republic are definitely monarchical traits. And some of the Soviet republics are, indeed. So, I see in monarchy a political doctrine which has nothing to do with dynastics, with crowns, with titles, with all that which I consider to be historical trappings. We have to go back to the origins from which the kings stem. The monarchical concept still has a role, but that doesn't mean dynasties and crowns and so on, but the political idea as such.

Q.:   On that point, you are perhaps more particularly relevant to Austrian life and people than other royal successors are to their particular countries, because in

Austria, particularly the German Austrians had no special national grouping of their own and they owed most of their direct loyalty to the Habsburgs.

O.v.H.:   Exactly.

Q.:   Certainly in sharp distinction to the other peoples in the empire. Do you not feel that this puts you in a specially relevant position to Austria?

O.v.H.:   At least as far as relations toward Europe are concerned specifically. We can really act as a catalyst because we have been less poisoned by the nationalism of the nineteenth century than others.

Q.:   I suspect that constitutionally now there would be no hindrance about your becoming, say, president of Austria.

O.v.H.:   President—I couldn't become. That is constitutionally laid down. I could run for any other office but not for the presidency.

Q.:   Would you ever consider taking public office on any level in Austria?

O.v.H.:   I wouldn't exclude it, if I thought it might be useful. For the time being I am not thinking of anything in particular. Now say for instance if we really succeed, which I think we may, in obtaining the popular election of the Austrian delegates to the Council of Europe—that might be a type of job I might be interested in—I *could* be interested in, say.

Q.:   We've talked mostly in terms again of *supra*national structures. What sympathy do you still feel with the calls of nationalism, or national minorities?

O.v.H.:   Well, concerning the national minorities, I would say that the supranational solutions are the only ones that will finally eliminate the problem. As long as we have national states, as long as a state and a nation are identified, minorities always will be in a position of inferiority. It is only in supranational organizations that you can create that equality of nationalities which will finally put an end to the minority problem.

Q.: But at the same time, thinking back to Austria-Hungary, it was the claims of nationalism which in fact broke down the empire.

O.v.H.: Yes, but this may be a personal view of mine—all these political forms have some sort of a mission in history, and I think that the old empire performed its mission in that sense, that it was the only one that held the supranational idea through the nineteenth century, when all the others were in nationalism. It *had* to fail because it was standing against the principles of the nineteenth century. But I do feel that the fact that it was able to last into the first part of the twentieth century, when the reverse trend began to set in, provides instruments with which to begin to rebuild something which was again supranational.

Q.: This again is rather in the realm of fantasy: if by any chance a monarchy of kinds was restored in Austria, or you took office again on something like that level, would you greatly miss the life of a private citizen?

O.v.H.: I would say probably yes, very much so. You see, there are some tremendous advantages when you can say what you want.

Q.: And you do effectively say what you want.

O.v.H.: Oh, yes, I say whatever I like.

Q.: You feel that there is no sort of dogmatism on your part which prevents you from speaking your mind?

O.v.H.: I don't think that there is very much. You see, I am saying it, I am writing it—this weekly column I am

writing on all sorts of questions is quite a pleasant
thing to do.

Q.: You have no sensation of slight heresy when you constantly embark on a pan-European ideal which *seems*
to an outsider perhaps to conflict with the old . . .

O.v.H.: No, I don't think it does. You see—after all, Charles
the Fifth and all the great figures of the past, figures
of my own family, were always rather supranational
in their approach. You see, for instance, I had the opportunity of writing a life of Charles the Fifth, which
took me ten years to do, and I would say that one
thing that struck me, for instance in his correspondence, was that he always used to speak of his *orbis
europaeus christianus*—let us say that the European
idea already existed then.

Q.: In terms of Europe again, do you see Europe as a buffer between East and West?

O.v.H.: No, I see Europe not as a buffer but as an independent
force in the world. You see, after all, numerically we
are stronger, even in the limited area of Western Europe; we are stronger than the Americans, we are more
numerous than the Russians; our economic potential
is very superior—if we were not still living in the states
of the nineteenth century, we would be just as much
a world power as, say, the Americans or the Japanese
or the Chinese.

Q.: Your concern is primarily European. Do you still feel
great connection with the United States?

O.v.H.: Yes, I go there quite frequently—I have done quite a
bit of lecturing in the United States.

Q.: Because you *did* work quite closely with President
Roosevelt.

O.v.H.:   Yes, at the time, and since that time I have always maintained very intimate contact with the United States. I go there at least twice or three times a year—often though for very short things, say for twenty-four hours. Every second year I do a lecture tour in the United States to keep a little bit in touch with the reality there.

Q.:   And you still maintain contacts on a fairly high political level.

O.v.H.:   Yes—in Washington there is scarcely a person whom I wouldn't know.

Q.:   Before you were allowed to return to Austria, I gather that Pocking was a place of, if you like, pilgrimage for Austrian legitimists and people who supported the old regime.

O.v.H.:   Yes—not only legitimists but others too.

Q.:   Did you change this or does it still happen?

O.v.H.:   No, not here, not in Pocking. People now can see me whenever they want in Austria. When I come here it is to do all my writing, this enormous correspondence I have, then all the different works I am doing, and consequently this is a sort of an office building almost. I see people when I am in Austria, which is about half the week. Soon it may be more. I hope so.

2) INTERVIEW WITH PRINCE LOUIS-FERDINAND

March 1972

QUESTION: I came to find you today in Berlin, and I was wondering whether there is anything symbolic in the fact that the present Hohenzollern should live in Berlin, the old Prussian capital.

Prince Louis-Ferdinand: Well, I think quite so. Because you know we are the oldest Berlinian family. My family came here from southern Germany during the fifteenth century, and we have lived here for about five hundred years.

Q.:   And do you find that the Berlin of today is a very different city from the Berlin you knew when you were young?

P.L.F.:   No—the people are the same. But the situation is unfortunate and different.

Q.:   If one was to say what is your occupation, how would you reply?

P.L.F.:   Well, you see I have really reached the retiring age—I'll be sixty-five this year. I once was asked by the [then] governor of Michigan, Soapy Williams, what business I was in, and I said in the pretender business, and he said, well, does it pay, and I said I don't quite know *yet!* So that would be the answer to this. . . .

Q.:   What sort of activities fill your everyday life?

P.L.F.:   Well, we have a sort of an administration for the rest of our fortune, which consisted mostly of land and woods and that's all east of the Elbe and was expropriated. But we still have a few shares, and I am interested in trying to keep that together, you see, because we have quite a lot of pensioned employees whom we take care of and we pay appanage to members of our family—that takes up quite a lot of my time.

Q.:   Are there any hereditary duties which you still discharge? Are there any ceremonial occasions on which you still appear in your capacity as head of the house of Hohenzollern?

P.L.F.:   Well, in a way, perhaps. We built this house, my wife and I, to have a center here in Berlin of communication, and we have concerts here once in a while—we just had the famous Argentinian pianist Bruno-Leonardo Gelber. He played here, and we have had very famous singers. So we invite our friends from all the political parties, and musicians, and we have a very nice crowd.

Q.:   Do people still address you in your royal capacity?

P.L.F.:   Yes—it depends perhaps on their political standpoint. But many say "Imperial Highness" or many say just "Prince Louis" or even others say "Louis," like the Americans generally call me by my first name. It doesn't make much difference, you know. But I must say we have a very nice atmosphere here in Berlin. We are considered as one of them, you know. That makes me very happy.

Q.:   To go back a little while; in a way you became head of the House of Hohenzollern by default, because your brother, your elder brother, married a com-

moner in 1935, I think. How did this promotion suddenly affect your life? Did it have a profound effect?

P.L.F.:   Well, yes, in a very definite way because I planned on
staying in the United States—I had emigrated really;
I had an emigration visa, so it only would have taken
me one or two years to get American citizenship. I
had it renewed up to the last moment until I got
married. I always could have gone back. But then I
said—no, no.

Q.:   Would you have been happy to stay in America?

P.L.F.:   Probably yes. But my marriage so definitely changed
my whole life and made me very, very happy. I don't
think I would have found somebody like my wife
there. But I still love America and I feel very much
at home there when I go back—I was there last year;
I visited my sister in America. It takes me only about
half an hour to get resettled, to get the American atmosphere right away. For me it's like a second home.

Q.:   Do you have a favorite memory from your royal childhood?

P.L.F.:   Well, the years in Danzig, where my father was the
commander of a cavalry regiment—that was really my
childhood. We spent three years there and that was
very, very happy—lots of outdoor life, and my parents
could also lead what was for those days a very un-
hampered existence. Whereas here in Berlin we were
always more closed in, you see.

Q.:   Your father had, I believe, all his properties confiscated during the Second World War.

P.L.F.:   No, not during; after.

Q.:   Did this put you in a financially awkward situation?

P.L.F.:   Well, certainly—at the beginning, extremely awkward for everybody. But then we still had some shares in West Germany, and these shares still existed. But at the time we wouldn't have survived without Care packages from the States—I've got to state that very strongly—from my friends who themselves didn't have much.

Q.: The old Prussia which one knew in imperial days doesn't exist any longer today, and many, very many Prussians are now in West Germany—live in West Germany. Do you feel particular ties to them, and are you perhaps a focal point for emigré Prussians in the West?

P.L.F.: Well, I am perhaps the most prominent expellee, if you want to say so. And I have very friendly relations with all these people, and I go to their meetings . . . of course this West Berlin is really the last part, the last free part, of Prussia.

Q.: Would you say that many of them are still monarchistic today?

P.L.F.: I think so, yes—they had several polls here in Germany and—well, the percentages have varied from thirty percent and less than that. But it went right across the party setup.

Q.: Your younger brother Frederich George has been quoted as saying that the return of the monarchy is "a remotely conceivable possibility in these days of political fantasies."

P.L.F.: Well, you see, I always say nothing is impossible in politics. I mean, who would have thought of President Nixon going to Peking a year ago? So things may happen. I wouldn't say it's certain, but I think the whole future is so completely uncertain, anything may happen.

Q.:   On the level of imagination, if a monarchy were restored, to what extent would you miss your private
life?

P.L.F.:   Well, probably very much. I believe in a United States
of Europe. That is not my *hope*; I am *convinced* that
it's going to come. And that certainly is going to re-
duce the sovereignty of the partner states—there may
not be a complete integration like the United States,
but it'll be similar, and it will be a federal setup with
the existing countries, but with a head as president.
I suppose you spoke to Otto about that because that's
his pet dog. . . . The part of the dynasty in such a
unit won't be so very glamorous any more. But it could
be very useful. Now, you see, even Britain is joining . . . they are keeping the monarchy for the time
being, and the same thing in Denmark.

Q.:   In other countries, where there are pretenders or
claimants to the throne, in Europe, how do you rate
the chances of a return of the monarchy?

P.L.F.:   Well, I would rate the chance of Juanito as the number one chance—Franco apparently wants it, and that's
it right now, and the army too—I think he's the closest
to that. How long he will remain—extra question!

Q.:   During the war you took part in the July plot to overthrow Hitler, although this political view wasn't
shared by your entire family; your uncle was a National Socialist deputy.

P.L.F.:   No, the family as a whole was anti-National Socialist,
anti-Hitler—there was only poor uncle Auwi. But they
didn't like the idea of conspiracy, or call it high treason, because they were brought up to believe in my
country right or wrong. And such a thing never had
happened during my family's rule.

Q.:   You were involved politically then; to what extent

have you been involved politically in Germany since the war?

P.L.F.:   I have no reason to be against anything—I'm on very good terms, well, with Willy Brandt, for instance—I just saw him three weeks ago. When he was mayor of Berlin, for the wedding of my daughter Marie Cecile he put the whole castle of Charlottenburg at our disposal. And not only that, but he also came. So as long as we have a democratic government, and a free democratic government, I am in favor of it—I'll never work against it.

Q.:   You've said that your ultimate idea for Europe is a united Europe, and you obviously believe in supranationalism. On a broader level, may I ask you how useful you feel the U.N. is as a political instrument?

P.L.F.:   . . . I would wish to see it much more active, much stronger, but . . . it's impossible for the time being.

Q.:   You're living here in Berlin with a communist country literally on your doorstep. Do you feel that communism on an international level is gaining or losing at the moment?

P.L.F.:   I don't think it's gaining. I don't see the monolithical aspects. In Russia there are great problems and there is a movement of freedom there, especially the young generation of writers and authors. I don't think that the Dubceks are going to diminish. I spent a week in the Soviet zone last year—August—and I spoke to many people. Especially for the young ones Dubcek is the symbol. They are not so much impressed by the western capitalism or by big bankers or people like that. The whole financial situation for them is not primary; they want to be free to talk and free to travel.

Q.:   Was that your first visit to the East since the war?

P.L.F.:   Yes, to the Soviet zone. I had been to eastern countries before then, on air rallies—Yugoslavia, Bulgaria, Hungary, and Rumania.

Q.:   Flying is a particular interest of yours.

P.L.F.:   Yes, I'm still a pilot—not very active any more, but I have a Cessna 182. I started my first lessons in Hollywood, you know.

Q.:   Really!

P.L.F.:   Yes, forty-five years ago. And then in Argentina I got my first license. So I'm now one of the veterans. We have an organization here in Germany that's called Alte Adler—people from the First World War. And now there's a book going to be published in London by a man called Mr. Birch, *Kings and Captains*, and it's about all the royalty who were aviators or RAF people. My granduncle Henry, who was an admiral and a great sportsman, had the first pilot's license of any royal member in the world.

Q.:   What did you fly before?

P.L.F.:   Well, during the war I flew a JU52. I'm a member of an organization called International Order of *Characters*—it's an American organization! It's more of a joke but it has a charity idea—the support of widows and children of flying personnel. In every country there are about thirty or forty members, and we get together. The governor [former] of Arizona, Goldwater, is a very prominent member. He's a most charming person. I met him and I didn't find him at all radical—I mean, as we would call, fascist. He's a right-wing liberal, I would say, as far as Germany would be concerned. He's about sixty-three—not much younger than I am—and he still flies jets, and has all his ratings. I don't have, I have only the PPL.

Q.:   Can I ask you some questions about your family—
       you have four sons and three daughters—how do you
       feel being Hohenzollerns has affected them?

P.L.F.:   [to Christian Sigismund] Well, *you* can answer that!

C.S.:   Well, we have been educated very freely, and there
         haven't been many problems for us, because people
         who don't know us are a bit respectful at first, but
         when they get to know us they see we are not different
         from them, and that makes the problems very small.

Q.:   Where do you all go for your holidays?

C.S.:   We have no *special* places.

P.L.F.:   Well, when we were living in Borgfeld [Bremen] we
           went to the North Sea islands quite a lot. Then we
           went to Spain, to Majorca, to Calpe—my children all
           love Spain, my wife too, she spoke Spanish quite well.

Q.:   And what are popular family activities—I think that
       music is very much in the family . . .

P.L.F.:   Well, he [Christian Sigismund] plays the accordian.
           And some of us love horseback riding.

C.S.:   And I'm interested in water sports.

Q.:   Two of your sons, your two eldest sons, have married
       commoners. How anxious are you that a third or a
       fourth son should marry a noncommoner in the in-
       terests of Hohenzollern continuity?

P.L.F.:   *Very* anxious—extremely. . . .

Q.:   The fact that they married commoners doesn't reflect
       a nonconcern of yours?

P.L.F.:   Oh, no, certainly no, but . . .

Q.:   Your daughter, of course, married . . .

P.L.F.:   She married one of the Oldenburg family. The others
           aren't married yet, but we'll see . . .

C.S.: We are not pressed for time!

P.L.F.: Of course my sister Cecilia married an American, Clyde Harris; he was an exceptionally nice person, very gifted, and it was a tragedy that he died much too soon. That wrecked her whole life.

Q.: Going back to America once again, in the 1930s you were a salesman and a mechanic for the Ford Motor Company, and you were extremely friendly, in a rather public way, with Lili Damita.

P.L.F.: Yes!

Q.: That's a long time ago. Now your autobiography, when published in English, appeared under the title of *Rebel Prince*. Do you still at sixty-five feel that you are a rebel prince?

P.L.F.: Well, I didn't invent that title—an American friend of mine, he thought that that would be a bit more exciting. You see, I was a rebel more or less . . . it doesn't quite apply, this word. It was considered so, I mean my attitude, but certainly my grandfather didn't regard me as a rebel. It sounds a little bit arrogant, but I was about forty years ahead of my time. Now all this has come, so I am no longer a rebel.

C.S.: Perhaps my father's point of view was a bit unknown at the time.

P.L.F.: You see, in those days to say that America was going to be the strongest country in the world and that it was extremely necessary to get together with her was considered a *heresy* here—you only went there if you had lost too much money! [Laughter]

Q.: Or came from Sicily! [Laughter]

P.L.F.: Now they overdo it, I think—poor America has to be responsible for everything. Of course that makes me laugh sometimes—people who are talking about America. But then, now they say America is going to the dogs because they are going to have another civil war; from my viewpoint that's all nonsense—it's completely normal. Of *course* they have the same symptoms as we have here. I still believe I know more about America than most people here.

Q.:   You say your *grandfather* didn't consider you to be a rebel—you mean the Kaiser?

P.L.F.:   The Kaiser. Because he was very broadminded and he was very modern, you know; he had the *vision* of . . . I think it's a damn shame that he never went to the States, because if he had, there *certainly* wouldn't have been a war, because the Americans would have *adored* him, and he the same way—they would have reciprocated beautifully.

Q.:   But in fact he never got there.

P.L.F.:   They wouldn't let him. But he knew many Americans —and the Kaiser-Wilhelm-Gesellschaft was a sort of copy of the Carnegie Institute—they exchanged professors and all that, and he got on very well with Teddy Roosevelt.

Q.:   The Kaiser-Wilhelm-Gesellschaft continued after his death?

P.L.F.:   It still exists now; they call it Max Plank Gesellschaft, because some of the Germans thought they didn't want to hurt the feelings of the victors of the war. But I'm sure nobody would have said anything. Knowing the Americans . . .

Q.:   You have *particular* affection, obviously, for America. What was the first thing that prompted you to go there?

P.L.F.:   Well, that was to follow Lili Damita! [Laughter] I wanted to know America, but that was the external reason. But then I got to know it and—that's how fate works, you see—Lili Damita disappeared out of my life, but America remained. Forever.

Q.:   Would you say that your position has been an advantage or a disadvantage in living your life?

P.L.F.: Both. Of course I have had many advantages and I still have. But there's one thing now—we have very few privileges, none practically. We are just as subject to public interference, by press. . . . We have no *rights* more than anybody else, but, let's say, if we want to get some theater tickets, or some other things, or if we travel on the Lufthansa or Pan American, we get VIP treatment, you know; we don't have to ask for it.

Q.:   And has this been so ever since you returned to Germany?

P.L.F.: From when I returned from America? Oh, yes. Even during the Nazi days—not by the Nazis themselves, but by all the others who weren't. And the Nazis didn't dare touch us, because as long as the German army existed . . .

Q.:   Did the fact that your uncle was a sympathizer to the Nazi cause in any way perhaps help you?

P.L.F.: Perhaps. I don't know. Our standing was so strong, you see, especially with the German army . . . well, that's why Hitler kicked us out, you see, because he thought after winning the war he could say "these didn't fight for the fatherland, and so we can treat them like this. . . ."

Q.:   Have you an ambition to see again your ancestral Prussian lands in East Germany?

P.L.F.: Of course I'd love to go. I can go to the Soviet zone any time, and you can go to these parts now under Polish administration—Pomerania, and East Prussia. But I think all these iron curtains are going to fall down—or bamboo curtains or whatever. *Tourism* is just going to roll over them.

P.L.F.:   [On the makeup of a state] The important thing is the *contents*.

Q.:   You mean the sort of people who make it up, and what they do.

P.L.F.:   No—if it's a republic or a monarchy, all right. But it must above all be a *free* country, and a prosperous one, and a liberal one, a tolerant one—that's what I would think is *the main* thing. I believe that for Germany probably a monarchy would still be the best thing, for the German state of mind, the mentality.

Q.:   It's curious, isn't it, that after a succession of *single* concepts—the monarchy, and Bismarck, and Hitler— quite suddenly there's a great even plain, with no particular height. I mean, to an outsider, German politics appear very . . .

P.L.F.:   Dull.

Q.:   Dull, and without a firm line, somtehing strong to grasp. Which seems to me contradictory, that it doesn't suit the German frame of mind—that German people *prefer* to have something quite clear to follow, something which represents their ideals, and not just a spread of political parties who have no particular strong point.

P.L.F.:   But perhaps it *suits* them. They like leadership, pageantry. I don't know. I only can tell from these visits of foreign queens or kings or shahs or Sorayas or . . .

Q.:   Or Kennedy?

P.L.F.:   Or Kenndy, a pseudomonarch. Incidentally, of course the American president has much more power than the kaiser ever had.

Q.:   Visitors to Germany seem to have an enormous attraction for German people.

P.L.F.:   They feel a gap within themselves. Hitler played to that gap and in that way Hitler was a pseudomonarch. The absence of the monarch is the gap. I talked to Lloyd George several times about it, and he realized that it was a great mistake to get rid of my family. And Churchill admitted it too.

3) INTERVIEW WITH DOM DUARTE

(Translated from German original)
March 1973

QUESTION: Although you're in Lisbon today, you usually live at Coimbra?

Dom Duarte: Yes, near Coimbra.

Q.: But you haven't always lived there.

D.D.: No—only for the last couple of years since we've been able to return to Portugal. Then we all came to San Marcos—that's its name. And then later my children came to Lisbon, for school, and I remained there. And then two years ago my wife died and so since then I've been mostly there alone, except when my children can come to visit me.

Q.: What are your children doing at the moment?

D.D.: Well, the eldest son happens to be here at the moment—he moves around quite a lot. He is in the middle of his studies at the University of Geneva, but has holidays just now. And then in a week he will go to Brazil, where he's been invited for a visit. My second son is on his military service in Mozambique, near Lourenco Marques. And the youngest is here—he was too young for military service.

Q.: Before your return to Portugal, where did you live?

D.D.:   In Switzerland, since shortly before the beginning of the war. And then from there I made one trip to Brazil, where I married a great-granddaughter of dom Pedro (emperor of Brazil). In this way the two branches of the family are reunited.

Q.:   Talking of Brazil, the Braganzas were Brazilian emperors for the greater part of the nineteenth century. What connection do you still have with Brazil?

D.D.:   Well, two of my wife's brothers are still there. And a sister.

Q.:   But you yourself don't have much contact with Brazil?

D.D.:   No, not really.

Q.:   What's the constitutional position of the Braganza family in Portugal now?

D.D.:   The Braganza family now is just my branch of the family.

Q.:   Yes, but what's your, so to speak, *legal* position—do you still retain, for example, your title of "Royal Highness"?

D.D.:   It is often used, but I don't think *legally* in the Republic . . . I'm also officially called duke of Braganza. But mostly "Royal Highness" also. And monarchists address me as "Your Majesty."

Q.:   Is there still a significant number of monarchists in Portugal today?

D.D.:   Yes, there's a fairly large number of them still. How many, it's difficult to tell. Perhaps a fifth who are *publicly* monarchists, but there are certainly more who sympathize.

Q.:   Do you still appear in your official capacity publicly?

D.D.:   It used to be more so—now, above all since the death of Salazar, or the disappearance of Salazar, much less, indeed hardly at all. I live mostly very quietly in San Marcos.

Q.:   We talked about Brazil—how do you feel about the Portuguese colonies? You don't call them colonies in Portugal. . . .

D.D.:   The provinces. Well, if I ever had the opportunity I would happily go, and I think I would be regarded by monarchists there in the same way as I am here. And then my eldest son especially, who served there for two years as a soldier—he is almost more African, more Angolan, than European! Because he loves the country very much.

Q.:   So the provinces really are a very important part of Portugal. . . .

D.D.:   Yes, very important.

Q.:   For every Portuguese?

D.D.:   Yes, really. But this wasn't recognized so, much earlier. However, the fact that we have come under attack there has greatly sharpened national awareness—today everyone takes it for granted that the provinces are an integral part of Portugal.

Q.:   What obligations does your royal position still carry on?

D.D.:   Well, no official ones. I should say that monarchists regard me as a sort of "father." But otherwise nothing.

Q.:   Do you feel that your position is an advantage or a disadvantage in living your life?

D.D.:   Personally, it's naturally a disadvantage, a great dis-advantage—it restricts me in many things. On the other hand, there's the satisfaction of fulfilling one's duty, which you find in all kinds of duty. But otherwise it's clearly a disadvantage.

Q.: Your eldest son will be your successor. Do you think that this is already something big in his life?

D.D.: Yes, it's certainly significant for him. He also considers it as a duty. And because he's very active, he's doing more now in this concern than I am able to do. But he sees it solely as a duty—he would certainly be very happy if someone were found to take this over from us!

Q.: What are your favorite hobbies or pastimes?

D.D.: Well, earlier I naturally had other ones—I used to fly, for example; I got my flying license in England. Less as time went on; I studied agronomy—I'm a graduate in agronomy from Toulouse, and I'm naturally very interested in that. Now I mostly do lighter work, writing and so on. And visiting. But mostly writing—that's how things have been for the last few years.

Q.: What do you think of the current chances for monarchy in other European countries?

D.D.: I'm perhaps not informed enough to really speak about this. I think, though, that in those countries where monarchy has been long established, it still seems to be the most *feasible* form, the best form of state. And of course there is also the fact that monarchy would be, for example, for us, but for others even more, the *cheapest* form of state. The very difficult and costly system which the United States has—scarcely any European country could afford it. Of course, those countries that have been without a monarchy for a long time now would find it very difficult to restore one.

Q.: What do you think of the chances of the restoration of the monarchy in Spain?

D.D.:   Well, I had more hopes for it until recently. But now General Franco, in choosing the young prince, has, so to speak, jumped over the king, his father, and thereby in fact has damaged the fundamental principle of monarchy—that it goes from father to son. And he has also largely ignored the people in this affair. And all these different factors—they will make things very difficult for this young prince after the departure of Franco. I very much fear that he will not be able to rule as king.

Q.:   What are the advantages that monarchy can offer in the 1970s?

D.D.:   The succession, the security. The continuity that a republic can never give. It's said that a prince is educated for the throne—that's not wholly the case, but he knows from the very beginning that he has this duty. While a general or a scientist who is elected president, for example, he has to learn this, and then in a couple of years he's gone again, and the same thing starts all over again, with parties and so on. A republic is always much more *costly* in these countries, because it is less *certain* than a monarchy. So the main advantage of monarchy is in fact the hereditary system, the continuity.

Q.:   During the last thirty years, Portugal and Spain have been quite close politically—during Spain's isolation from Europe, Portugal was almost her only friend, and the Iberian pact between Salazar and Franco of the 1930s was renewed in 1970, I think. What connections and friendship do you feel with Spain?

D.D.:   I think that—perhaps it has something to do with race —almost every Portuguese feels some friendship for Spain, but at the same time usually feels a little afraid of Spain. Because Spain is significantly larger, and in fact has never really abandoned the idea of incorporating *this* part of the Iberian peninsula. Because of that there is this fear. Otherwise, of course, there are very many similarities.

Q.:   You say that Spain is larger. But the posters in Lisbon show maps of Portugal and the provinces superimposed on the rest of Europe, and the total area is enormous. When you think about Portugal, do you think simultaneously about the provinces, in the way people in the nineteenth century thought simultaneously of Britain and the empire?

D.D.:   Yes, I think I've always thought that way, and now many others too, as I mentioned earlier, largely because of the attacks, and the need for defense that follows from them—the troops, and the many young men who make them up; the whole country has again become very aware. In the time of the discoveries this feeling was certainly very strong, a great awareness of the overseas provinces. And then this was rather forgotten for a while. But now the feeling is there again throughout the country. When we lost a very small, though important, part of our overseas provinces in India—Goa—it was a national sorrow; it was as if a great big part of our country had been taken away from us. That was about five years ago.

Q.:   We spoke just now of Spanish isolation. But Portugal is in almost the same situation—perhaps it's an Iberian situation. Do you believe that Portugal can remain isolated, especially economically, from the rest of Europe?

D.D.:   I think that this will slowly change. A certain distance, separation, will always remain. But there will certainly be an approach, especially through the much greater movement of people—travelers and so on. Many young people who come here will leave with an impression not that Portugal is something completely foreign and strange but that it is beautiful, a little old-fashioned perhaps, but a beautiful country. And that they're proud that it is part of Europe. I've often heard that, from German, French people, and Swiss, and so on.

Q.:   In 1932 you were suddenly recognized as the official claimant. But you were already twenty years old then —did it make a change in your life?

D.D.:   Hardly—things didn't change very much. Because the Miguellists had never recognized the "liberal" king— they only recognized my father, and subsequently me. Otherwise things didn't change much either, because we were abroad, and in Portuguese law we were still prohibited from setting foot on Portuguese soil—on pain of death! That law dates back to 1834.

Q.:   When did you first hear that this law had been abolished?

D.D.:   Well, we could in fact come—my sister earlier, and then later myself; it was still officially illegal, but possible. And then Salazar commissioned lawyers to reexamine the situation; they were republicans of course, but they reexamined the matter, and then they discovered that the law, which had deprived my grandfather Miguel of Portuguese nationality, was completely invalid. It had been enacted by a foreigner, and it was invalid in every respect. So we had spent over a hundred years in exile, without possessions or anything, because of a law which wasn't even valid! And I believe—this is perhaps a rather personal view —that the government didn't want to emphasize this too much, because they were afraid that I might demand the return of all the things that had belonged to my grandfather. But it was officially recognized and accepted by everybody that I was the only Portuguese heir, and that in fact we had never lost our Portuguese nationality.

Q.:   So then it was naturally clear that you could return. When you returned, however, you didn't have any possessions?

D.D.:   No, and I *still* don't.

Q.:   You mentioned Salazar just now. Did you ever meet him?

D.D.:   We didn't ever meet—I never talked to him personally. But otherwise I had very good relations with him, although naturally only indirectly.

Q.:   And since his death, are you still in some contact with the government?

D.D.:   Well, after Salazar's death an excellent, earlier protégé of his took over, but I couldn't tell exactly what his reactions would be, so I've been living very silently and quietly, in my country house. I've really done very little. Only recently, however, the minister president met my son and appeared very sympathetic toward us. Since then, I've become more active about our affairs. Before that I was a little afraid of political problems.

Q.:   You mention republicans when you talk about Portugal. But surely Portugal is hardly a true republic—perhaps for the same reasons that made the Spanish republican experiment such a failure.

D.D.:   Yes. For example, a country that I like and know very well—Switzerland—they are republicans deep down inside, because they've always had that feeling. But there is a very great difference between a Swiss and a great Portuguese republican, you know, because even when he believes and says that he is a republican, he isn't one really. He's a bad republican!

Q.:   Your eldest son is about twenty-seven now, but not married yet. From the point of view of the House of

Braganza, how necessary do you think it is that he should marry a noncommoner?

D.D.: Well, I believe, not only because this is something I was taught but also from my own experience, that it would certainly be better for him and his descendants if he were to marry someone from a noble family.

Q.: Is this something historical?

D.D.: It's really something racial—it occurs in so many cases in nature, for example, in horse-breeding and other things, where the great-grandparents and so on can always be exactly traced in their descendants. Because one knows that for certain purposes it is very much better when you control the breeding succession. And it's the same with humans.

Q.: What sort of role would you like your son to play when he succeeds you?

D.D.: Well, the head of the royal house, although as I said before, my sons share my feeling that this is a duty rather than a pleasure, or any personal desire. He will continue this task, and certainly much better than I. He has built up a great many friendships and acquaintances recently in Portugal, and in the last while also in Brazil. He has been invited there twice already officially, by the government—with everything paid and so on.

Q.: By the *government?*

D.D.: Yes, officially, and as I say with the advantage that everything was paid, because we aren't rich! And he was very happy to go.

Q.: And in what capacity was he invited?

D.D.: As a descendant, through my wife, of dom Pedro, the last emperor of Brazil.

Q.: So he has a double connection—not only your connection with Portugal, but also a growing connection with Brazil.

D.D.: Yes—this was always one of Salazar's wishes, and for a long time he pursued a very gifted and careful politics aimed at removing this separation from Brazil and bringing Brazil much closer again. The same problem existed with Spain and he solved it quite quickly. With Brazil it took a long time, but now it's already very far advanced. . . . Of course Brazil has many things which we don't have. But we can give bases in Africa, and in Europe, and other things too. Exactly as a father, who already may have given his possessions to his son, still has many other things to offer. And perhaps one of the most important gifts is that Brazil can claim a history which goes back six hundred years, to Portuguese beginnings. And they are therefore very proud that they are descended from Portuguese ancestors. And of course now increasingly there are reciprocal arrangements about citizenship and passports and so on, which bring us closer together.

Q.: Can you tell me about this fund of the House of Braganza?

D.D.: Well, it was created after the death of Manuel, and it was created by Salazar so as to gather together the remaining Braganza possessions and prevent any more being lost. This was about 1945. You see, the House of Braganza, in earlier history, was founded by a younger brother of a king of Portugal, and the family lived, so to speak, parallel with the royal family, and was fairly wealthy and had many possessions. And then when there was no king, the duke of Braganza was called, and became king. But his personal possessions remained intact, and were kept for the use of his family and were not allowed to be sold.

Q.:   Does the present fund include a lot of buildings?

D.D.:   I don't know them all. It also includes a great deal of
             land—good land, which is well managed. From the
             legal point of view, once it was established that in
             fact we had never lost Portuguese nationality and
             that this law was invalid, we considered that we should
             really have also received our possessions back again.
             But that hasn't happened yet.

Q.:   But you have San Marcos.

D.D.:   It has been, so to speak, placed at my disposal. It
             doesn't belong to me. I also receive a small sum of
             money, which at the beginning was fine but now,
             with rising prices, is hardly sufficient.

4) INTERVIEW WITH DON JUAN
March 1972

QUESTION: Well, first of all, I'm going to ask you, sir: Estoril has been your center of activity for a very long time, since the forties?

Don Juan: Since forty-six. During the war I stayed in Switzerland. And then I thought that I would like to come closer to Spain, to be more in touch with my own people, so therefore I decided to come to Portugal. It's been very agreeable, and I have stayed here—I see no point in going elsewhere! But I travel a lot—every two or three months I go to Paris, Rome, London, the States . . .

Q.:   Do you feel that Estoril is a home?

D.J.:   Well, we needed a base; we've got lots of things; we can't be traveling the whole time without a fixed home!

Q.:   Estoril has always, especially during the war and even now, been a center for foreign royalty.

D.J.:   Well, I think it became so little by little. I was the first to come! [Laughter] Then later on came the King of Italy, and then came the Count of Paris. He went back to France when the law against his exile was lifted. And then—we also had here the King of Rumania, the father of Michael who is the king now. He died here. King Carol. So then we were a little bunch.

163

But I think it has been mostly because Portugal is a very nice little country and quiet, I mean we are not so much in the public eye continually—it would be difficult to keep out either in Rome or Paris or London.

Q.: There's a scene in Voltaire's *Candide*, when he's in Venice, and there's a group of five very distinguished-looking men at the next table in a restaurant, and he asks them who they are, and they say they are five kings in exile, and it seems to me Estoril is a bit like that! [Laughter] It was very shortly before his death, wasn't it, about a month before his death, that your father renounced his rights in your favor?

D.J.: A month before he died. He felt he was dying, and he wanted to have things already settled and with the acceptance of all my brother and sisters and so on.

Q.: And did this make a sudden change in your life?

D.J.: Not really, because he had already nominated me his heir in 1933 when my elder brothers renounced. The elder because he married a commoner, and the second one because he was a deaf-mute since he was born.

Q.: Well, since then you've been constantly active in Spanish affairs—ever since then. Have politics in Spain completely consumed your life? Does it take up your whole time?

D.J.: Not the whole, but a great deal of it. But now, since three years I have suspended my public activities in politics.

Q.: Since 1969?

D.J.: Since then. I thought that—well, I won't go *against* the situation; I feel that the monarchy is difficult enough as it is, and to have two monarchs, I mean, well!

Q.:   Have you enjoyed politics during your life, or have you been involved in them really as a dynastic obligation?

D.J.:   Out of a sense of duty. I can assure you, politics are no fun! And especially not this kind.

Q.:   So it's been a sense of obligation, really.

D.J.:   Yes, obligation—to our birth, to our country, to the institution we represent.

Q.:   What about your pastimes? I gather you're a great yachting man.

D.J.:   Well, I was a sailor since I was very young, because I was not the heir—I went into the navy very young, at fifteen, in the Spanish navy. And then when the Republic came in 'thirty-one, I passed over to the British navy—to the Royal Navy.

Q.:   To the *Royal* Navy!

D.J.:   Yes. I was six years in the Royal Navy. And I'm still in the navy list! I am an honorary lieutenant—I didn't go up very much!

Q.:   And you still keep up great interest in yachting? I gather you're going to Kiel.

D.J.:   Yes, but then my father also was a yachtsman, and we started very young in sailing boats and I've loved sailing ever since. During the war, in Switzerland, I even had boats on the lake! [Laughter] To keep it up.

Q.:   What about the rest of your family—do you see much of your daughters?

D.J.:   Well, one lives with me, the youngest. She's going to marry this year, possibly. And the other one married four years ago, and she had lived with me until she married. And my eldest son—well I have two; one died here, and the eldest one goes and comes—every two or three months he comes for a week or so, with children and so on. My grandchildren are sweet.

Q.: So this is very much a family home.

D.J.: This is the base. And then there is the telephone!

Q.: How strong are your contacts now with people and places in Europe?

D.J.: Well, I know more or less the politicians in every country—I talk to them, at meetings and things like that.

Q.: And on a social level as well—you travel quite a bit?

D.J.: Yes, I don't go officially, but . . . they like to hear one's point of view and I like to hear theirs!

Q.: You mentioned that now, since 1969, things have changed. What's your day-to-day life made up of at the moment?

D.J.: A lot of reading, a lot of . . . going through information that comes to me from Spain, because I keep up my information—to keep it up the same as ever. I'm in touch with people, the same as ever—the only thing is I don't do anything public. There hasn't been a great change in my life; I've got sailing in the summer, I've got golf in the winter, a little shooting also!

Q.: There are no ceremonial occasions on which you still appear in public in, say, a royal capacity?

D.J.: Well, I went to the funeral of King Frederick in Denmark, and things like that.

Q.: What does it feel like to be a pretender? A claimant?

D.J.: That's a funny one! Well, you see, we were born in this . . . business. But I don't consider myself a pretender and I don't pretend anything that I don't think I have a right to!

Q.: It's a ridiculous word, actually—it's one of the strangest words in the English language!

D.J.: It's *such* a strange word, I've always gone against it, all my life—I don't pretend anything! I *am*! for the people who recognize, and for the others—nothing!

Q.: How is social life in Estoril?

D.J.: Quiet. Very quiet. I've got a group of friends—different—sporting friends—things like that, and we have dinners, reunions, lectures . . . I like concerts also; they've got a good concert hall in the Gulbenkian.

Q.: I'm going to ask you some questions about Spain. Ever since 1945 you've been an apparent champion of the cause of liberalism.

D.J.: That, I can assure you, that's the truth! [Laughter]

Q.: I'm quoting from something you said in 1969—something that appeared in *Le Monde*: "il faut que la monarchie soit aussi la representation authentique du peuple et que la volonté nationale soit presente dans tous les organismes de la vie publique . . . La societé doit pouvoir s'exprimer librement par les moyens normaux d'expression . . ."

D.J.: Ce sont des choses qu'on peut pas dire en Éspagne!

Q.: Absolument! But this was the source of your first, if you like, conflict with Franco in 1945, when you issued your manifesto and so on. . . . And you really repeated it then in 1969—you were saying, "this is something which I've said for thirty years."

D.J.: Well . . . I never *fought* with General Franco, really; to be honest, we've had differences of opinion. He believed in totalitarian government; he believed that his regime, with what they call an "organic representation," was sufficient, and this might have worked if the war had gone differently—if Italy and Germany had won the war. But obviously it was impossible when they lost the war. Therefore a change was necessary. We were very fortunate in Spain that the *so-called* democracy, parliamentary democracy, was a terrible fiasco during the Republic.

Q.: Why, in *your* opinion, was the Republic such a disastrous failure?

D.J.: Well, because it gave way to all the bad feelings that the Spaniards have, without any sense of authority or of duty. They divided themselves up into small parties and made national politics impossible—for *any* government or chief of state. There were a hundred and thirty-nine governments in five years!

Q.: Well, surely you've touched there on one of the great problems for *any* Spanish government—whether it's republican or monarchical or totalitarian—and that is this tremendous splintering.

D.J.: Splintering—yes—it's happening now in Italy.

Q.: Well, especially in Spain you have this tremendous regionalism—there's a great tendency for things to fall apart.

D.J.: And the reason I think is because they are more personal . . . the person who is at the head of an idea is more important than the idea. People follow—the groups form—around a *personality*. Much more than for what he says—probably the man next door is saying the same thing, but they like the other one more!

Q.: So from a political point of view the Spaniards are really very immature?

D.J.: It's difficult, always been very difficult. But it's a question of education—they've never been *allowed* either.

Today I would think that the country is fully pre-pared to go into a European type of political life.

Q.: You think it's prepared?

D.J.: Well, there are extremes on left and right, but I think there would be a very large center.

Q.: From the outside one has always seen that Spanish politics have been an affair of extremes.

D.J.: Extremes, yes. And that's what makes these types of military governments nearly necessary.

Q.: I'm going to again throw quotes at you—you spoke then [1969] of "la societé doit pouvoir s'exprimer librement et par les moyens normaux d'expression" and you spoke of "libertés collectives et individuelles." And this is something which General Franco said in 1967 in his address to the nation—he said that one may not "tolerer aucune opposition—institutionalisée, car celle-ci est une opposition déloyale."

D.J.: The idea of opposition in this regime is nonexistent. So that as soon as you put yourself in the opposition, either you are Red or . . . something like that. There is no alternative, and that's why it is so uncomfort-able . . . there is no community life between the real Spain and the political papers. There is a divorce there between people and government.

Q.: Well, I think the divorce is maintained by the fact that the government has never, during the last thirty years, leaned on the *people* for its support.

D.J.: No. They haven't needed public opinion. There is a *silent* public opinion—you see, the civil war was a very cruel affair, and the generation, say, from my age upwards—well, they still remember, and they *support* a great deal of . . . imposed law. But the younger ones who have no inkling of what that war was, and who don't feel it in the same way as we do—surely they are not going to think like that.

Q.: This is really a question of political science: in *all* totalitarian regimes the greatest problem, political problem, is always the question of succession, because a totalitarian regime has no inherent concept of legitimacy—it has to create its own. And Franco is obviously very concerned to ensure his succession.

D.J.: He is concerned always with that, because . . . all dictators want to perpetuate themselves! And they know they're not eternal. They have to find some propitiation. So that's probably why they thought that my son, who had been more or less brought up in this atmosphere, wouldn't have the independence that I had. But it's going to be very difficult anyhow.

Q.: It is going to be difficult?

D.J.: Yes, because, though there's been a referendum . . . referendums are done and one still doesn't really know.

Q.: One of the problems seems to be that, because of the way things have happened, Juan-Carlos is necessarily identified with *Franquisme*.

D.J.: Yes.

Q.: Franco has deliberately made this so?

D.J.: That's what's happened exactly. And I always felt that the institution (monarchy) should not identify itself with any political nomination—it's *above* that, and that's precisely how it can subsist in the countries where there still are monarchies, because they are above the parties—they don't belong to one . . .

Q.: Monarchical sovereignty must be something completely above normal political life?

D.J.: It's a *representation* of the state, it's a *continuity*, it's a statement of a possibility to counsel from the inside, and then, to represent the country, without . . . changes.

Q.: When I was with Otto von Habsburg we were talking about legitimacy, and he said, and I think you might agree with this, that the trouble about legitimacy is that it's such an *intangible* thing. And that it very rarely outlives the generation which has seen its end.

D.J.: Exactly. And that's why, to quote my own self, I have often said that the ligament, the connection, between crown and country has to be renewed, to create that very legitimacy again. Because otherwise it will be broken, broken by revolution—it happened in France, it happened everywhere, and now in Spain—well, it's already forty years ago since the monarchy is out—that's three generations. So that you need a popular vote in favor of the restoration of the monarchy again—if not, you have no authority. I have always stressed very much upon that point.

Q.: Yes, indeed—you're certainly quoting yourself! You said in 1969, about the law of 1947 and its application—you said in 1969: "On ne m'a pas consulté et on n'a pas solicité l'opinion librement exprimée du peuple espagnol."

Q.: In 1968 you went to Madrid.

D.J.: Yes, when my grandson was born.

Q.: And your mother . . .

D.J.: Yes, she was the godmother.

Q.: Outside Spain, people made comment on the fact that there was a very significant welcome for you then—a popular welcome—and that you yourself had private audiences with several important members of the regime. Which was in sharp contrast to your visit to Madrid two years before that.

D.J.:   Which had been a hush-hush affair.

Q.:   And suddenly two years later you come quite publicly, with a public demonstration and so on . . .

D.J.:   Well, that was partly wanted, and partly not organized, because we didn't make the people go anywhere, but they just did, *spontaneously*. The government . . . they were horrified!

Q.:   And in fact they were so horrified that there were due to be celebrations for the feast of San Juan, and they were stopped.

D.J.:   They stopped it! And . . . it's very difficult to say how many people there were, but without previous announcement, and without organization, just by people telling each other—well, there were over fifty thousand people in that aerodrome, and the yells and shouts—you could hear them. That you don't invent!

Q.:   I hadn't realized there were so many people there.

D.J.:   It impressed me also—I didn't expect it.

Q.:   This again is something you said in 1969—"Je continue à croire en la necessité de l'evolution pacifique vers une ouverture et une pratique démocratique, qui est l'unique garantie d'un avenir stable pour notre patrie." But at the same time the continued attitude of the regime is that a public opinion may not be tolerated. Does that make you pessimistic about this "avenir stable"?

D.J.:   *Very* pessimistic! Very pessimistic, because the stability is only given by the unique authority of General Franco.

Q.: It's been quite stable for a long time—which is rare in Spain—thirty years.

D.J.: But things are starting to move—take the Church movement, take the student movement, take the workers' movement—there were dead people the other day in Ferrol; all the universities are closed down today. . . .

Q.: You mention the Church there, which brings me to ask you about the unique position of the *opusdeistas* for a long time in the government, in the whole hierarchy of Spanish life. Their political thoughts would seem to be to halt any move toward liberalism, while at the same time to concentrate heavily on economic development.

D.J.: Yes—they are all the technologists.

Q.: It would seem then that if *Franquisme* can continue after Franco, it would be a sort of technocratic-military regime.

D.J.: Well, it's very difficult to predict the future. But what is pretty clear is that nobody is going to have the moral authority to have a supreme command after Franco, as Franco has had. That is sure. And therefore I think the military and the armed forces and police and all that will maintain the legality of the constitution as far as it can, but it's going to come from inside [i.e. not from the people]. . . . It has worked now so far because Franco commands himself, without anybody going against him.

Q.: Have you met Franco since 1960?

D.J.: I met him in 1968 also.

Q.: What was the atmosphere at that meeting?

D.J.: Well—he was cold, he was cordial. . . .

Q.: Can I ask you about the army—your father had a life-long attachment to the army, and Juan-Carlos has quite a military education, and the army is very much a pillar of this regime.

D.J.: Well, you know, the military education that is usually given to princes—you have seen that even Prince Charles has gone through the armed forces—is mainly due to . . . first, to have a contact with the forces that are going to be on the side of peace, and that in time of war will have to represent the country in fighting. But also because it disciplines your mind and body; I think that's the main thing.

Q.: But the army in Spain is in a very special position— Fraga Iribarne [minister of information until 1969] has stressed this several times. In 1965 he said "quoi qu'il arrive, les forces armées continueront à être garantes de la situation, et aucune solution ne sera possible sans leur consentement." Which seems to place an enormous *political* decision in the hands of the army.

D.J.: Well, constitutionally they can be obliged to take up the position of being the guarantee of the regime—*la ley organica*, as they call it. How far that can go—the army is also the people!

Q.: Can we move away from Spain for a moment and talk about Europe? The applications of Spain to the EEC have been consistently refused. Surely it's going to be very difficult, though, for Spain to remain economically isolated from Europe?

D.J.: Not only difficult—disastrous. We are all frightfully preoccupied about this, and as long as the institutions are based on what they are now, it will be impossible for us to go into the Common Market.

Q.: Both on political and economic grounds?

D.J.:   It's mostly political—one can jump over lots of the economic difficulties.

Q.:   How do you feel about Spanish involvement with the United States?

D.J.:   Well . . . it isn't so much as one thinks. You see we had to stay on one side and we can't go over to the Russian side so easily, so one had to stay on the western side!

Q.:   How do you rate the United Nations at the moment as an effective instrument?

D.J.:   Well, I don't think I should give my opinion of the United Nations—I think it has been a very . . . generous proposition, but in its results, very poor. They have passed on all the defects of democracy in each country to democracy between countries which are not on the same level! No one pays any more attention!

Q.:   For thirty years the Spanish state has appeared as a champion of the cause of anticommunism. Do you feel that communism internationally is gaining or losing?

D.J.:   I would say there is an evolution even in Russian communism. I think for export they have certain ideas, but not . . .

Q.:   Two kinds of communism—export and domestic!

D.J.:   And domestic! Yes!

Q.:   To talk about monarchy again—how do you feel about monarchy in the rest of Europe? Do you think the prospects are good anywhere else in Europe?

D.J.:   Well, they are—I think they're fairly good. New instalments are difficult—now we've got the Greek regime there, it's taking long to arrange . . . I don't think I'm wrong if I say that essentially it's a good regime [monarchy], like all other regimes if they are well applied and if they've also got the support of the people. You can't invent a monarchy in the United States . . . but nearly they approach it also, with their prolongation of their presidents!

Q.:   Would you say that your position has been an advantage or a disadvantage just in living your life?

D.J.:   I should say a disadvantage. Disadvantage in the way that I arrive nearly to my sixty years old and I have been sort of always on the verge of having to do my duty without anything behind it.

Q.:   Do you have many regrets?

D.J.:   Regrets—no. I think if one's got a clear conscience . . . I've tried to do my duty to my country, and to myself, and to what I represent, and I think that everybody recognizes. And that's a moral satisfaction. The question of success is always in this world so adapted to the circumstances that one never knows when it is real success or not.

Q.:   How do you see the next few years passing?

D.J.:   Well, I think we are going to see some changes in the next few years—biological ones at least! [Laughter]

Q.:   Biological ones!

D.J.:   Well, somebody's got to die soon! [Laughter]

Q.:   A quotation from Salvador de Madariaga—"L'Espagnol est un spectateur."

D.J.:   Well, there is a lot in that. I mean, you see it in sport, and everything—the country is more a spectator than an actor. For instance, in sport—you find very few people who play football, but they know *everything* about football to criticize and to watch. In bullfighting you have people who wouldn't know how to take a cape in their hands but they know *everything* about it! And that's why the number of our sportsmen is very, very, very small—because they prefer to be spectators than to be actors.

Q.:   And they are self-appointed critics?

D.J.:   Yes, they are essentially critical. And very unconstructive very often! Because it's easier to criticize, in a café, what the minister for finance is doing, but one wonders what he would do if he was minister for finance!

Q.:   That relates to another quotation from Madariaga, about the problems which this creates for getting Spain organized, getting any sort of constructive politics in Spain—"ce qui est discutable, ce n'est pas seulement la capacité qu'ont les Espagnols de s'organiser en *état,* monarchique ou republicain, mais leur capacité de s'organiser en *nation.*"

D.J.:   That's at the basis of the problem. That's why the monarchy has always had a very good influence in that question of becoming a nation—for instance, my title, Count of Barcelona; I took it up with the *idea* of it being recognized, because it's such a region—Catalonia. Their natural señor is the Count of Barcelona—the king of Castile they don't like so much! [Laughter]

Q.:   I remember reading about the Spanish-American empire, and the great thing there that strikes one, and I get the impression it's still true today, is the *regionalism*—that it wasn't Spain that conquered America, but *Castile.*

D.J.:   Well, the union was very recent. King Ferdinand and Queen Isabella—well, she was a Castilian and he was an Aragonese-Catalan. He wasn't interested very much in the American business, and he concentrated on the

Mediterranean—his ideas were Mediterranean—Sicily, Naples, Milan, Sardinia. Whereas the queen thought of going to populate and create other countries. . . . But the generosity of the Cortes was enormous, and it created, gave way to this anarchical sense that the Spaniards have. There was no local authority—they could do more or less what they thought in each place, and that's why you've got such different countries in all South America: it's like a picture of Spain!

Q.:   Quite changing the subject—you mentioned that the universities are closed today. How do you feel about young people in Spain?

D.J.:   Well, I don't think they are honestly bad. There is a sense of frustration, egged on of course by underground politics. . . . The great mass of people would like to be able to study properly and to have a proper teaching. But I think also there is a lack of authority, *academic* authority—for instance, people that don't go to classes . . . and then the *structure*—sudden expansion of the scholarship system in Spain has been a bit too fast for the universities themselves. Look—from twenty-one thousand in 1958 to 1960, we've gone up to sixty thousand in this year. And the lists of professors has augmented only five percent, or something like that. So they have to double up the classes, but with people who are not really prepared, it's unsatisfactory.

Q.:   So apart from political control, the academic standard is not what it might be.

D.J.:   Exactly. And if you get a student eighteen or twenty years old who can teach the professor—well, it's a bad thing!

Q.:   The other day there was an enormous wedding in Madrid, with its great publicity in the newspapers.

[The marriage of Franco's granddaughter, Maria del Carmen Martinez Bordui y Franco, and don Juan's nephew, Prince don Alfonso de Borbon y Dampierre]

D.J.:   Yes. I am just receiving the papers now. I would prefer not to comment.

Appendices

ROYALTY-WATCHERS' EXERCISES

APPENDIX A *Brief Historical Synopses of Claimants'*
Royal Houses

Ardent royalty-watchers eventually get mesmerized by the glittering
tangle of royal family histories, and are often found deep in history
books tracing doggedly the warp and woof of the monarchial fabric.
To capsulize these histories is to synthesize them into bones without
flesh. As a mere catechism of lineages, however, the following fragments
may provoke the royalty buff to further pursuit.

THE KINGDOM OF ALBANIA

HOUSE OF ZOGOU
His Majesty King Leka I

The royal house of Albania is the House of Zogou (Zogolli). The
house is Moslem by religion and stems from an important Albanian
family prominent since the fifteenth century in northcentral Albania.
The family is descended from the Zogolli, heroes of Albanian independence, who fought against the Turks. During the Turkish occupation
of Albania, the descendants of the Zogolli were hereditary governors
of Mati Province and succeeded each other for generations. After the
defeat of the Turks, the son of Xhemal Pasha Zogou was proclaimed
King Zog I of Albania in 1928, having been elected in 1925 president
of the Republic, and hailed as one of the architects of Albanian independence. Zog's son, King Leka, is the current claimant.

THE EMPIRE OF AUSTRIA AND THE KINGDOM OF HUNGARY

HOUSE OF HABSBURG-LORRAINE

His Imperial and Royal Highness Archduke Otto of Austria and King of Hungary

The House of Habsburg descends from Gontran the Rich who lived in the tenth century and who was lord of Muri. His son Lantold-Lanzelin and his grandson, count of Altenbourg, built the Chateau de Habsburg in Argovie, and their descendants became counts of Habsburg. Rudolf of Habsburg was elected emperor of the Holy Roman Empire in 1273. His son Albert was duke of Austria and his descendants were hereditary sovereigns of Austria. The son of Maxmillian of Habsburg, emperor of the Holy Roman Empire, was Charles V (1500–1558). Upon Charles's death, the House of Habsburg divided into two branches: the kings of Spain with Philip II; the emperors of Austria with Ferdinand, whose issue became extinct with Maria-Theresa. Maria-Theresa was married in 1741 to Duke Franz III of Lorraine, who was elected emperor of the Holy Roman Empire. They are the ancestors of the imperial and royal House of Habsburg-Lorraine today. The present head of the house is His Imperial and Royal Highness Archduke Otto of Austria.

THE KINGDOM OF BULGARIA

HOUSE OF SAXE-COBURG AND GOTHA

His Majesty King Simeon II

The royal House of Bulgaria descends from the House of Saxe-Coburg and Gotha, itself a branch of the House of Saxe. This house is one of the oldest dynasties in Germany. It appeared in 919 with Thiademar, count of Dedo. Since then the House of Saxe-Coburg has been prominently involved with the establishment of a number of foreign royal houses: Great Britain, Belgium, Portugal, and Bulgaria. Ferdinand of Saxe-Coburg and Gotha became King Ferdinand of the Bulgarians in 1887. Ferdinand I abdicated in 1918 in favor of his son, King Boris III, who died in 1943—six years after the birth of his son, King Simeon, the present head of the royal house.

THE KINGDOM OF FRANCE AND THE FRENCH EMPIRE

1) HOUSE OF CAPET: ORLÉANS BRANCH

Monseigneur Henri d'Orléans, Count of Paris (*de jure:* Henri VI, King of France)

The royal house of France is descended from Robert the Strong, count of Paris, duke of France, who lived in the ninth century and whose grandson, Hugh Capet, was crowned king of France in 987. Capet's male descendants succeeded to the French throne without interruption for about four hundred years. In 1327 the senior branch became extinct in the male line, and the junior branch of the Valois line mounted the throne with Philip VI of Valois. This branch also became extinct in 1589, and the Bourbon branch was given the crown at the time of Henri IV.

The Bourbon branch of the family reigned until 1793, the year of King Louis XVI's death. After the interruption of the French Revolution and the empire of the Bonapartes, the Bourbons came back to France in 1814 with King Louis XVIII. Charles X, who was exiled in 1830, was succeeded by his cousin, the duke of Orléans, who reigned as King Louis-Philippe I until 1848 when the monarchy was overthrown and he fled to England.

King Charles X's grandson, the count of Chambord—known among the monarchists as Henri V—died without children in 1883, the last prince of the senior branch of the house of France. In accordance with French dynastic law, the head of the junior branch, Philippe, Count of Paris—referred to as Philippe VII—grandson of King Louis-Philippe I, became chief of the royal house. He was succeeded by his son, Philippe VIII, who died childless and was succeeded by his cousin, Jean, duke of Guise, known as Jean III, who became chief of the royal house. Jean, who died in 1940, was the father of the present head, Henri VI, the Count of Paris.

2) HOUSE OF BONAPARTE

His Imperial Highness, Prince Louis Napoleon Bonaparte

The imperial house of France is the House of Bonaparte. Originating in Genoa, it established itself in the sixteenth century in Corsica, where its members had various municipal positions of authority. Charles Bonaparte (1746–1785) was made a noble by the king of France when Corsica was rejoined to the kingdom of France. He married Letitia Ramolina, a local Corsican, by whom he had thirteen children —five of whom were boys. The second son, Napoleon, started the family on its illustrious climb—by becoming a general, first consul, and then emperor of France in 1804 under the name of Napoleon I. Having produced no heirs by his wife Josephine de Beauharnais, he married secondly Archduchess Marie Louise of Austria, who produced an only son, Napoleon II, king of Rome and duke of Reischtadt, who died in Veinna in 1832 without any heirs. Napoleon I's nephew, Prince Louis-Napoleon Bonaparte, was elected president of the Republic in 1848; he then reestablished the empire and was proclaimed emperor in 1851. As Napoleon III he lost his throne by a vote of the National Assembly in 1871, following the war between Prussia and France, and died in exile in 1873.

Napoleon III's marriage to Eugenie de Montijo produced only one son, Prince Louis-Napoleon, who was killed by the Zulus in Africa in 1879 without heirs. The present imperial house descends from Prince Jerome-Napoleon Bonaparte (1784–1860), the last brother of Napoleon I, who was king of Westphalia from 1807 to 1813. His eldest son, Prince Napoleon (1822–1891) became chief of the imperial house upon the death of Napoleon III in 1879. His son, Prince Victor-Napoleon (1862–1926), followed as head of the family and sired Prince Louis, who is the present chief of the imperial house.

THE EMPIRE OF GERMANY AND THE KINGDOM OF PRUSSIA

HOUSE OF HOHENZOLLERN

His Imperial and Royal Highness Prince Louis-Ferdinand of Prussia

The House of Hohenzollern had become feudal nobility by the middle of the tenth century. The Hohenzollerns were made burgraves (hereditary governors of a castle or town; counts) of Nuremberg by virtue of the marriage of Count Frederick with Sophie, daughter of the last burgrave of the House of Raabs in about 1200. The two sons born of this marriage are the ancestors of the present royal line.

The titles of prince of the Holy Roman Empire and margraves (marquises) of Brandenburg were conferred upon the Hohenzollerns in the fourteenth century. Conrad, count of Zollern and margrave of Nuremberg, was the direct ancestor of the present line from which came the kings of Prussia and emperors of Germany up to 1914. They became dukes of Prussia around 1600, kings of Prussia in 1700, and finally emperors of Germany in 1871 when Kaiser Wilhelm I federated the German principalities under his rule. The last king-emperor was his grandson, Kaiser Wilhelm II, who abdicated in 1918 after the German defeat at the end of World War I. The present claimant is the grandson of Kaiser Wilhelm II.

THE KINGDOM OF IRELAND

1) HOUSE OF CONCHOBHAR (Conor)
   The O'Conor don, the Reverend Charles Denis Mary Joseph Anthony O'Conor

The O'Conor don is descended from Conchobhar (Conor), king of Connacht (one of the four provinces of Ireland), who died in 971 and was the son of Teigh of The Three Towers, and eighteenth in descent from Daagh Galach, the first Christian king of Connacht in the fifth century. The last two High Kings of Ireland were of this line—King Turlough O'Conor (1088–1156) and King Roderic O'Conor (1156–1198). Roderic O'Conor was king of Connacht and supreme monarch of Ireland. The English invasion of Ireland in 1170 culminated in the Treaty of Windsor in 1175, whereby the kings of England became lords paramount of Ireland, and Roderic then held the kingdom of Connacht as a vassal of the English crown.

2) HOUSE OF BRIAN BOROIMHE (O'Brien)
   The Right Honorable Lord Inchiquin, Seventeenth Baron of Inchiquin, Sir Phaedrig Lucius Ambrose O'Brien

The royal House of O'Brien is one of a few native Irish houses now to be found in the English peerage. It is descended in an unbroken male line from Brian Boroimhe (Boru), king of Thomond (North Munster), who became supreme monarch or Ard Ri of Ireland in 1002, and was slain in battle at the decisive victory of the Irish over the Danes at Clontarf in 1014. King Brian Boru, from whom the family takes it name (O'Brien) succeeded a long line of kings and princes that came to an end as a reigning dynasty when Murrough O'Brien, king of Thomond, in 1543, was forced to surrender his royalty to King Henry VIII of England, and was created by him baron of Inchiquin and Earl of Thomond, ancestor of the current claimant, Lord Inchiquin.

3) HOUSE OF UI NIALL (O'Neill)
Fourth Baron O'Neill, Lord Raymond Arthur Clanaboy O'Neill

The dynastic House of O'Neill is accepted by some scholars as the oldest traceable family left in Europe. Its descent reaches back into the mists of pre-Christian Ireland when pagan Iron Age kings ruled the land. One of the ancestors, Eochu Mugmedon, king of Tara in A.D. 360, made slave raids on Roman Britain, in one of which he carried off and eventually married a princess of the ancient Britons, known as Carina, who produced his son Niall of the Nine Hostages. During the reign of High King Niall, starting about A.D. 400, the royal house had nominal sway over all of Ireland. A later King Niall was killed in a battle with Norsemen in A.D. 919.

Until the time of King Brian Boru (House of O'Brien), who reigned in the early part of the eleventh century, the Ui Neill—that is, descendants of Niall of the Nine Hostages—were High Kings of Ireland almost without interruption. The House of O'Neill remained kings of Ulster (the province in which Northern Ireland is located) for centuries, and have been involved with the affairs of that province ever since. The current claimant, Lord Raymond O'Neill, still lives in County Antrim; his uncle, Lord Terence O'Neill, was Prime Minister of Northern Ireland from 1963 to 1969.

THE KINGDOM OF ITALY

HOUSE OF SAVOY

His Majesty King Umberto II

The royal family of Italy issues from the House of Savoy. Its origin goes back to Umberto I, count of Savoy, whose hereditary sovereignty was recognized in the eleventh century by Emperor Conrad II. The Piedmont area in northeastern Italy was taken over in 1060 by Otto of Savoy. The counts—later dukes—of Savoy played important roles in the area's history. Perpetual vicars of the Holy Roman Empire with hereditary titles from the thirteenth century, they were princes of the Holy Roman Empire. In 1462 their rights to the kingdoms of Cyprus, Armenia, and Jerusalem were recognized. Duke Victor Amedeo II of Savoy received the kingdom of Sicily in 1718, and exchanged it for the kingdom of Sardinia in 1720. The eldest branch of the house became extinct in the male line in 1831, and the junior line, called Savoy-Carignan, succeeded it. It is from this line that the present royal family comes.

Victor Emmanuel, King of Sardinia, was the architect of the unification of the Italian peninsula, and became King of Italy in 1861, as Victor Emmanuel II. His grandson was King Victor Emmanuel III, father of Umberto II, the present head of the royal house.

THE KINGDOM OF PORTUGAL

HOUSE OF BRAGANZA

His Royal Highness dom Duarte Nuño, Duke of Braganza

The royal house of Portugal is the House of Braganza, which is descended in a direct line from the Capetians of France. The king of France, Robert II the Pious, who died in 1031, was the son of Hugh Capet, and produced several male heirs. Henry I, the eldest, was the "founder" of the royal house of France. The second son, Robert, duke of Burgundy, was the father of Henry of Burgundy who conquered Portugal in 1703, and became, in turn, the father of Alphonse I, king of Portugal and founder of the royal house.

The Portugese royal house is divided into several branches—Aviz and Braganza which reigned until 1910 when the throne was lost.

After the struggles that in the nineteenth century divided the partisans of King Miguel I and those of dona Maira II, a reconciliation between the two branches took place in 1920, followed by the death in 1932 of Manual II, who had no heirs. The grandson of King Miguel, Prince dom Duarte Nuño, duke of Braganza, became head of the royal house, thereby uniting the dynastic rights of the two branches.

THE KINGDOM OF RUMANIA

HOUSE OF HOHENZOLLERN-SIGMARINGEN
His Majesty King Michael I

The royal house of Rumania stems from the Hohenzollern-Sigmaringen family which ruled Prussia. Both branches are descended from Frederick of Zollern who was the ruling noble of Nuremberg in the thirteenth century. The Sigmaringen branch, the oldest line of Prussian kings, produced a number of princes of the Holy Roman Empire who reigned, until 1849, over the principalities of Hohenzollern-Hechingen and Hohenzollern-Sigmaringen. Prince Charles, who took the name of Carol I, ruled Rumania from 1866 to 1914. Upon his death, his nephew, Prince Ferdinand of Hohenzollern-Sigmaringen, succeeded him as Ferdinand I from 1914 to 1927—when his grandson Michael succeeded him as King Michael I, the present head of the royal house.

King Michael's father, Carol, was in exile when the young sovereign came to the throne. He returned to Rumania in 1930 and was proclaimed King Carol II. He reigned until the Germans forced his abdication ten years later, during the early part of World War II, and Michael became king for the second time.

THE EMPIRE OF RUSSIA

HOUSE OF ROMANOFF-HOLSTEIN-GOTTORP
His Imperial Highness Grand Duke Vladimir Cyrilovitch, Grand Duke of Russia

The imperial House of Romanoff inherited the throne of Russia from the House of Moscow, descended from the famous Chief Rurik, who established his dynasty in Russia in the ninth century. His descendants were grand princes of Moscow. Ivan III freed Russia from Mongol domination at approximately the same time as Christopher Columbus discovered America. Ivan III's grandson, Ivan the Terrible, was the first Czar of All the Russias (1530–1594). After some years of internal strife, Michael Romanoff was proclaimed czar by a National Assembly convened, after the expulsion of the Poles from Moscow in 1613, for the purpose of establishing the nearest of kin to the old dynasty whose direct male issue terminated with the death of Theodore I in 1598. Michael Romanoff was the grandnephew of Anastasia, first wife of Ivan the Terrible and mother of Theodore I. According to the Byzantine views on succession prevalent in Russia at that time, Michael was the nearest legitimate heir. After the demise of the last of the direct-line Romanoffs (Empress Elizabeth in 1761), the imperial crown passed to her nephew, son of her sister Anne and the duke of Holstein-Gottorp, who ascended the throne as Czar Peter III.

The last czar, Nicholas II, was assassinated with all his family in 1917. His cousin, Grand Duke Cyril Vladimirovitch, grandson of Czar Alexander II, and eldest of the Romanoffs, became head of the imperial house and was recognized as such. The present head of the family and claimant to the throne is his son, Grand Duke Vladimir of Russia.

THE KINGDOM OF SPAIN

HOUSE OF BOURBON-ANJOU

1) His Royal Highness don Juan of Bourbon and Battenburg, Count of Barcelona
2) His Royal Highness don Juan Carlos of Bourbon and Battenberg, Crown Prince of Spain, Prince of Asturias

The royal house of Spain today is the House of Bourbon-Anjou. It stems from the houses which previously reigned over the kingdoms of Castile, Leon, Aragon, and Navarre, and which were united by their Catholic Majesties, Ferdinand I of Aragon and Isabella of Castile (who financed Christopher Columbus's voyages to the New World). Their only daughter, Jeanne, married Philip the Handsome, son of Emperor Maximilian of Habsburg. Charles II was the last of the House of Habsburg to be king of Spain. Upon his death, having no children, his grandnephew Philip, duke of Anjou, was designated as heir. Philip was the grandson of King Louis XIV of France and his queen, Marie-Theresa, eldest sister of Emperor Charles II of Austria. With King Philip V, the Spanish House of Bourbon was formed as well as the royal House of Naples and the ducal House of Parma.

When King Ferdinand VII of Spain died in 1833, after having abolished the Law of Succession of 1713, there was a civil war between the supporters of the legitimacy (who demanded the throne for the brother of Ferdinand VII, Charles V, and who were known as Carlists) and the liberals (who were partisans of Isabella II, daughter of Ferdinand VII). Isabella II married Prince François d'Assise de Bourbon, nephew of Ferdinand VII and Charles V. This marriage produced Alphonso XII, father of Alphonso XIII, king of Spain from 1885 to 1931. The last Carlist pretender, Prince don Alphonso-Charles I, died without heirs in 1936, and his rights to the throne were reunited to those of the junior branch represented by the present chief of the royal house, don Juan of Bourbon and Battenberg, count of Barcelona.

THE OTTOMAN EMPIRE

HOUSE OF OSMAN
His Imperial Highness Prince Osman Fuad

The Osman (Othman or Ottoman) dynasty began with the tribe of Ogrul which came from the Transcaspian steppes of modern Uzbekistan (USSR) and settled in Eastern Turkey in the thirteenth century. Within one hundred years the House of Osman had become emirs and finally sultans by conquering their previous rulers, the Seljuk Turks.

By the time of the reign of Sultan Suleiman I (1520–1566), the Ottoman Empire was the foremost power in Central Europe extending its authority and influence to North Africa, Eastern and Western Europe, and to the frontiers of Western Asia. Internal problems, rebellions, and disastrous political and military alliances weakened the Ottoman Empire until the last sultan, Mohammed VI, was deposed in 1922.

The current claimant, who bears the name of the founder of the Royal House, is His Imperial Highness Prince Osman Fuad, the grand-nephew of the last Sultan of Turkey.

THE KINGDOM OF YUGOSLAVIA

HOUSE OF KARAGEORGEVITCH

His Royal Highness Prince Alexander

The royal house of Yugoslavia descends in a direct line from George Petrovitch Karageorges, who succeeded in expelling the Turks in 1804. Karageorges was made hereditary prince of Serbia in 1808. His grandson became Peter I, king of the Serbs in 1903, and was succeeded by his younger brother, King Alexander I of Yugoslavia. Alexander was assassinated in Marseilles in 1934. He left three sons, the eldest of whom became King Peter II, the father of Prince Alexander, the present claimant.

Appendix B *Other Crowns and Other Claimants*

In addition to the eighteen claimants described above, there are six others who dynastic claims are valid, and taken seriously by themselves, their fellow claimants, and in some cases, by monarchist sympathizers in the respective territories concerned. I have set the six apart from the others, not because of lesser validity of the claims, but merely because the countries whose crowns these claimants represent are no longer separate national entities: The kingdoms of Bavaria, Hanover, Saxony, and Württemberg (now parts of Germany), the Kingdom of the Two Sicilies and the Duchy of Parma (now parts of Italy).

These claimants are closely related to the other royal houses. Their houses and families have provided marriage partners for the reigning and nonreigning royalty of Europe for centuries—and they continue to do so today.

THE KINGDOM OF BAVARIA

THE HOUSE OF WITTELSBACH
His Royal Highness Prince Albert of Bavaria, Duke of Bavaria

Otto V the Great, Count of Wittelsbach, was made duke of Bavaria in 1180 by Emperor Frederick. The royal Bavarian house provided several emperors of the Holy Roman Empire. Maxmillian-Joseph of Bavaria became the first king of Bavaria in 1805. The present chief of the royal house, Prince Albert, is the son of Prince Rupprecht of Bavaria and the Duchess Marie-Gabrielle, sister of Queen Mother Elizabeth of Belgium. Albert became the claimant upon his father's death in 1955, and was recognized as king by the Bavarian monarchists.

Prince Albert of Bavaria is married to the former Countess Marie

Draskovich de Trakostjan and has two sons and twin daughters: Prince Francis (thirty-nine), Prince Max-Emmanuel (thirty-two), Princess Marie Gabrielle (forty-two), married to Prince George de Walburg à Zeil et Trauchburg, and Princess Marie Charlotte, married to Prince Paul de Quadt à Wykradt et Isny.

THE KINGDOM OF HANOVER

HOUSE OF BRUNSWICK-LÜNEBURG

Prince Ernest-Augustus of Hanover, Duke of Brunswick and Lüneburg, Duke of Cumberland, Royal Prince of Great Britain and Northern Ireland.

The royal House of Hanover descends from the ancient family of Guelphs whose heirs were dukes of Saxony and Bavaria in the eleventh and twelfth centuries. The family became connected in 1714 with the royal house of Great Britain by virtue of the marriage of the Hanoverian Duke Ernest-Augustus with Sophie, daughter of the Holy Roman Empire's Frederick V and Princess Elizabeth of Great Britain and Ireland, who was of the English House of Stuart. Ernest-Augustus, the uncle of Queen Victoria of England, took the crown of Hanover in 1837, and was followed by his son King George V of Hanover who had the Kingdom taken away from him by Prussia in 1866. George's grandson, Ernest-Augustus, was able to recover the duchy of Brunswick in 1913 but was forced to abdicate in 1918.

The present claimant, Prince Ernest-Augustus was born in 1914 in Brunswick, Germany, the eldest son of Prince Ernest-Augustus and the former Royal Princess Victoria-Louise of Prussia. He was recognized as King Ernest-Augustus III by the Hanoverian monarchists upon the death of his father in 1953, two years after his marriage to Princess Ortrud of Schleswig-Holstein-Sonderburg-Glucksburg who is related to the Danish royal family. Prince Ernest-Augustus (fifty-seven) and Princess Ortrud (forty-six) have three sons and three daughters— all of whom were born in Hanover and whose ages range from twenty to eleven years.

THE KINGDOM OF SAXONY

HOUSE OF WETTIN

His Royal Highness Prince Frederick-Christian of Saxony, Margrave of Misnie, Duke of Saxony

The royal House of Saxony goes back to Count Thiadmar in the tenth century. Various branches of the house reigned in the duchies of Saxe, Coburg, and Weimar, and in the principalities of Saxe-Meiningen, Sax-Altenburg, and Saxe-Coburg and Gotha. Members of the royal family of Saxony have married into and are closely related to the royal families of England, Belgium, and Bulgaria. King Frederick-Augustus III of Saxony was forced to abdicate at the end of World War I, and his son Prince Frederick-Christian became head of the house and claimant to the throne of Saxony when he died in 1932.

Prince Frederick-Christian is eighty-two years old, and is the second son of King Frederick-Augustus III and Archduchess Louise of Austria. He is married to the former Princess Elizabeth-Helen of Thurn and Taxis, whose mother was Archduchess Marguerite of Austria. The princess and prince have two sons and three daughters. The heir to the royal rights is the elder son, Prince Emmanuel of Saxony (forty-five), who is married to Princess Anastasia-Louise d'Aubalt, a cousin whose family were also dukes of Saxony-Wittenberg in the twelfth and thirteenth centuries.

THE KINGDOM OF WÜRTTEMBERG

HOUSE OF WÜRTTEMBERG

His Royal Highness Philip, Duke of Württemberg

The royal House of Württemberg is an ancient and princely German family stemming from Conrad of Württemberg in the eleventh century. Over several centuries the house increased its sovereign territories by acquiring the lands of Urach, Calw, Teck, and Montbeliard. The Duke of Württemberg, Frederick II, became king of Württemberg. With the death of King William, the elder branch of the family closed, and the dynastic rights passed to the head of the junior branch, Duke Albert.

The present head of the royal house, Duke Philip of Württemberg, was born eighty-two years ago in Stuttgart. He is the eldest son of Duke Albert and the Archduchess Marguerite of Austria. Philip was married first to Archduchess Helen of Austria, a cousin, in 1923. who died ten months later. He then married Helen's younger sister, Archduchess Rosa of Austria, in 1928. The parents of Helen and Rosa were Archduke Pierre-Ferdinand of Austria, head of the grand-ducal family of Tuscany and Princess Marie-Christine of Bourbon, princess of the Two Sicilies.

By his first marriage, Duke Philip had one child, Duchess Marie Christine (forty-seven) who is married to Prince George of Liechtenstein, son of Prince Aloys of Liechtenstein and Archduchess Elizabeth of Austria.

Philip's marriage to Rosa produced four daughters and two sons. The eldest daughter married Margrave Frederic Pallavicini; another married Prince Antoine de Bourbon, prince of the Two Sicilies; and another is the wife of Prince Henri d'Orléans, who is the son of the claimant to the French throne, the Count of Paris, and his wife Princess Isabella of Orléans and Braganza, of the Portuguese royal house.

The eldest son, Duke Louis, was heir to the throne until his marriage to the Baroness Adelaide de Bodman. He renouncd his and his heirs' rights to the throne in favor of his brother, Duke Carl (thirty-six). Carl is married to his sister-in-law, Princess Diane d'Orléans (thirty-two).

THE KINGDOM OF THE TWO SICILIES

HOUSE OF BOURBON OF THE TWO SICILIES
His Royal Highness Prince Renier de Bourbon, Prince of the Two Sicilies, Duke of Castro

The royal House of the Two Sicilies, a junior branch of the heirs of Philip V of Spain, grandson of Louis XIV of France, was sovereign, independent, and separate from the royal house of Spain. The family reigned in Sicily and Naples from the early 1800s until King Victor Emmanuel of Italy proclaimed the kingdom of the Two Sicilies to be part of the kingdom of Italy.

Prince Renier de Bourbon is eighty-nine years old, and is the ninth child and fifth son of Prince Alphonse and Princess Marie-Antoinette de Bourbon, princess of the Two Sicilies. Renier is married to the former Countess Caroline de Saryusz de Zamosczamoyska whose mother, Marie-Caroline de Bourbon, was also princess of the Two Sicilies. They have a daughter, Princess Carmen de Bourbon (forty-seven), and a son, Prince Ferdinand de Bourbon (forty-five), the heir apparent.

THE DUCHY OF PARMA

HOUSE OF BOURBON-PARMA

His Royal Highness Prince Robert of Bourbon, Duke of Parma, Plaisance, and the Annexed States

The ducal House of Parma is a branch of the Bourbons descended from King Philip V of Spain. The younger brother of King Charles III of Spain, Crown Prince Philip, before inheriting the Spanish throne, received the sovereignty of the duchies of Parma, Plaisance, and Guastella by the Treaty of Aix-la-Chapelle in 1748. His descendants reigned —with interruptions by the Bonapartes and Empress Marie-Louise—until the mid-1800s when the duchy of Parma was annexed by King Victor Emmanuel at the time of Italy's unification. The duke of Parma was forced into exile in 1860 without relinquishing his dynastic rights or abdicating. The last reigning duke of Parma, Prince Robert of Bourbon, married twice and had twenty-three children. He is the ancestor of all the present princes of Bourbon-Parma.

The current head of the ducal house is his grandson, Prince Robert, who succeeded to the title upon his father's death in 1959. Prince Robert (sixty-three), the oldest son and third child of Prince Elie de Bourbon and the former Archduchess Marie-Anne of Austria, is a bachelor; the heir apparent to the title of duke of Parma is, therefore, his uncle, Prince Xavier de Bourbon, who is eighty-three years old and married to the former Countess Madeline de Bourbon-Busset. Prince Xavier has four daughters and two sons. The eldest daughter, Princess François (forty-four), is married to Prince Edward de Lobkowicz, of a feudal Bohemian family, and the eldest son, Prince Hughes (forty-two), is married to Princess Irene of Orange-Nassau, daughter of Queen Juliana and Prince Bernard of the Netherlands.

(To the above group could be added other claims and other claimants, such as: ANHALT (Prince Leopold Friedrich, thirty-four, descended from the dukes of Saxony); BADEN (His Royal Highness Prince Maximillian, margrave of Baden, thirty-nine, closely related to the Greek and Yugoslavian royal families); GEORGIA (His Royal Highness Prince Irakly-Bragration-Moukchranski, sixty-three, who is the brother-in-law of Vladimir, the Russian claimant, was once married to Her Royal Highness Princess de las Mercedes, the Infanta of Spain, and is descended from the ancient dynasty of Bagratides, which reigned in the Caucasus for over a thousand years and still has not renounced its royal prerogatives); HESSE (His Royal Highness Philip, landgrave and prince of Hesse, seventy-six, who married Princess Mafalda, second daughter of King Victor Emanuel of Italy); LIPPE-BIESTERFELD (His Serene Highness Armin, Prince of Lippe, forty-eight, whose cousin, Prince Bernhard, married Queen Juliana of Holland); SCHAUMBURG-LIPPE (His Serene Highness Wolrod, prince of Schaumburg-Lippe, eighty-five); MECKLENBURG (His Royal Highness Friedrich Franz IV, hereditary grand duke of Mecklenburg-Schwerin, sixty-two); MONTENEGRO (His Royal Highness Michael, Prince Petrovich Niegosch of Montenegro, sixty-four); and OLDENBURG (His Royal Highness Nicolaus, grand duke of Oldenburg, seventy-five).

(The territorial entities which these claimants represent have been folded into and, in some cases, digested by the larger nations of Eastern and Western Europe. Most are now part of Germany, several having seen the last of their sovereignties at the end of World War I in 1918. Montenegro is now a part of Yugoslavia, and Georgia was annexed by Imperial Russia, and is now a part of the USSR.

(The ancient royal house of POLAND—which ranks fourth in official antiquity among the royal houses of Europe—would seem to deserve listing with the major claimants: Poland as a country remains a national entity, and the descendents of the last sovereign are extant. However, since Poland's last king, Stanislaus II, in 1795, there has been no officially recognized claimant. The Poniatowski family, whose members descend from the feudal counts of Poland in direct line from Count Joseph, elder son of Count Franz, aide-de-camp to King John Sobieski III, represents the legitimate pretenders. But the Polish kings were traditionally *elected* from the royal family, and no individual from the Pontiatowskis has been universally agreed upon and tapped as the claimant.

(There are distinguished Poniatowskis in the United States, France, Mexico, Austria, Germany, and Holland. Probably the most logical "candidate" for claimancy would be Prince Philip Edmond Joseph Stanilaus, forty-eight, who married the Countess Irene Bonin de la Bonniniere de Beaumont, and lives in Seine-et-Oise, France.

(It may be unfair to the record not in include BRAZIL even though it means moving to another hemisphere.[1] The close ties of the imperial Brazilian family with the royal families of France, Portugal, the Two Sicilies, and Bavaria, however, make it appropriate to mention His Imperial and Royal Highness Prince Pedro-Henrique of Orléans-Braganza, sixty-three, head of the imperial Brazilian house. Prince Pedro is married to Princess Marie of Bavaria and has twelve children. His cousins Princess Marie Françoise and Princess Isabella are married respectively to the claimants to the Portuguese and French thrones. Pedro is the great-grandson of Emperor dom Pedro II who left Brazil in 1889 following a revolution.)

NOTES

1. While we are concerned solely with the empty thrones of Europe, the compleat royalty-watcher may want to know the current claimants to non-European thrones:

CLAIMANTS TO THRONES OUTSIDE OF EUROPE

COUNTRY	NAME	YEAR OF BIRTH	SUCCEEDED TO CLAIM	RESIDES	YEAR HOU DEPOSED
Afganistan	His Majesty Mohammad Zahir Shah	1914	1933	Italy	1973
Brazil	His Imperial Majesty Emperor dom Pedro III Enrique	1909	1921	Brazil	1889
Burma	*	–	–	–	–
Burundi	His Majesty King Mwambutsa IV	*	*	Switzerland	1966
Cambodia	Her Majesty Queen-Dowager Kossamak Nearireak	*	1960	Cambodia	1970
China	His Imperial Majesty Great Ts' ing Emperor Kung-hsu	(secret)	1967	(secret)	1912
Egypt	His Majesty King Ahmed-Fuad II	1952	1952	Switzerland	1953
India	(Grand Mogul)	*	*	*	1857
Iraq (including Syria & Lebanon)	His Majesty King Ra'ad	*	1970	Jordan	1958
Korea	His Imperial Majesty Emperor Kyu	*	1970	Korea	1910
Libya	His Majesty King Idris I	1890	1951	Egypt	1969
Madagascar	*	*	*	*	1896
Maldive Is.	*	–	–	–	*
Mexico	*	–	–	–	1867
Mongolia	*	–	–	–	1924
Rwanda	His Majesty King Kigeri V	*	*	*	1961
Tunisia	*	*	*	*	1957
Vietnam	His Imperial Majesty Emperor Bao Dai	1913	1935	France	1955
Yemen	His Majesty Iman Mohammed al-Badr	1928	1962	England	1955
Zanzibar	His Highness Sultan Jamshid bin Abdullah	1929	1963	England	1964

* Undetermined. Investigations in progress.

APPENDIX C *Present Royal and Reigning Families*

As all royalty-watchers know, the main attractions continue to be the sovereigns who have kept their crowns and their thrones. They are in the news, visible, and live in their own countries.

The reigning families are also basically the keepers of the monarchial flame in Europe as far as the claimants are concerned. And it is not merely a whimsical responsibility: The nine European royal families who are still in business have sovereignty over more than 185 million people. (The claimants, if restored to their thrones, would represent hypothetical sovereignty over 493 million people. A royalty-watcher with a statistical penchant could make an assumption that, therefore, the business of kingship in Europe is at about 27 percent of its capacity.)

No view of the claimants is totally clear without a glance at the survivors—the current royal and reigning families. They give a sanctuary of hope, a glimmer of reality to the claimants to Europe's empty thrones. The reigning familes are, for the most part, entrenched and popular, progressive and effective. The inter-relationships, kinships, and bloodlines between themselves and their nonreigning peers could be a powerful political bond in the matrix of a new Europe which is now taking shape.

THE KINGDOM OF BELGIUM

HOUSE OF SAXE-COBURG AND GOTHA
His Majesty Baudouin I, King of the Belgians

King Baudouin is forty-two years old and is married to the former dona Fabiola de Moray-Aragon, the daughter of the marquis de Casa Riera of Spain. They do not presently have children. Baudouin is the eldest son of King Leopold III and Queen Astrid, the former Princess Astrid of Sweden. King Baudouin has reigned since 1951.

THE KINGDOM OF DENMARK

HOUSE OF SCHLESWIG-HOLSTEIN-SONDERBURG-GLUCKSBURG
Her Majesty Queen Margrethe II

Queen Margrethe, thirty-two, came to the throne in 1972 upon the death of her father, King Frederick IX, who was the eldest son of King Christian X and Queen Alexandrine, the former Duchess of Mecklenburg. Margrethe's mother, Queen Ingrid, was princess of Sweden, the daughter of the late King Gustaf VI of Sweden and the Queen, the former Princess Marguerite of Great Britain and Ireland. Margrethe has two sisters—Princess Benedikte, twenty-eight, married to Prince Richard-Casimir de Sayn-Wittgenstein-Berleberg of Germany, and Princess Anne-Marie, who is now the queen of Greece, married to King Constantine II.[1] Queen Margrethe of Denmark is married to French Count Henri de Laborde de Monpezat (thirty-eight) and they have two small sons.

THE KINGDOM OF GREAT BRITAIN

HOUSE OF WINDSOR
Her Majesty Elizabeth II, Queen of the United Kingdom of Great Britain and Northern Ireland

Queen Elizabeth was born in London forty-five years ago. The daughter of King George VI and the former Lady Elizabeth Bowes-Lyon, she is married to Prince Philip of Greece and Denmark who is the son of Prince Andrew of Greece and Denmark and Princess Alice of Battenberg. Queen Elizabeth and Prince Philip have four children: Prince Charles, the heir apparent, Princess Anne, Prince Andrew, and Prince Edward. The Queen has reigned since 1952.

THE KINGDOM OF GREECE

HOUSE OF SCHLESWIG-HOLSTEIN-SONDERBURG-GLUCKSBURG

His Majesty King Constantine II, King of Greece, Prince of Denmark

King Constantine is thirty-two years old, the only son and second child of King Paul and Queen Frederika, the former Princess of Hanover. He is married to Princess Anne-Marie of Denmark, the daughter of King Frederick IX of Denmark and Queen Ingrid, princess of Sweden. King Constantine and Queen Anne-Marie have three children: Princess Alexia, Prince Paul and Prince Nicholas. He became king in 1964; Constantine and his family went to Italy for "temporary exile" in 1968.[1]

THE PRINCIPALITY OF LIECHTENSTEIN

PRINCELY HOUSE OF LIECHTENSTEIN

His Serene Highness Prince Franz-Joseph II, Sovereign Prince of Liechtenstein

Prince Franz-Joseph was born in Austria in 1906, the son of Prince Aloys of Liechtenstein and the former Archduchess Elizabeth of Austria. He is married to Countess Georgina de Wilczek, the daughter of Count Ferdinand de Wilczek and the former Countess Kinsky de Wchinitz and Tettan. The Prince and Princess have five children: Prince Hans-Adam (twenty-seven) who is married to Countess Maria Kinsky de Wchinitz and Tettan, Prince Philip-Erasmus (twenty-six), Prince Nicolas-Ferdinand (twenty-five), Princess Nora-Elizabeth (twenty-two), and Prince Franz-Joseph-Wenceslas (ten). The prince of Liechtenstein has reigned since 1938.

THE GRAND DUCHY OF LUXEMBOURG

HOUSE OF NASSAU

His Royal Highness the Grand Duke Jean of Luxembourg, Duke of Nassau, Prince of Bourbon-Parma, Palatine Count of the Rhine

Grand Duke Jean is fifty years old and is the son of Grand Duchess Charlotte of Luxembourg and her consort Prince Felix of Bourbon, prince of Parma. He is married to Princess Josephine-Charlotte of Belgium (forty-four) the daughter of King Leopold III and Queen Astrid of Belgium, the former Princess Astrid of Sweden. Their royal highnesses have three sons and two daughters. Grand Duke Jean has reigned since 1964.

THE PRINCIPALITY OF MONACO

HOUSE OF GRIMALDI

His Serene Highness Prince Rainier III, Sovereign Prince of Monaco

Prince Rainier is forty-nine years old and is married to the former Grace Kelly (forty-two), daughter of John Brendan Kelly and Margaret Meyer of Philadelphia. Rainier is the son of Princess Charlotte of Monaco, duchess of Valentinois, and Count Pierre Polignac. Their serene highnesses have two daughters and a son. The prince has reigned since 1949.

THE KINGDOM OF NORWAY

HOUSE OF SCHLESWIG-HOLSTEIN-SONDERBURG-GLUCKSBURG

His Majesty Olaf I, King of Norway

King Olaf (sixty-nine) was born in England, the only son of King Haakon VII of Norway and the Queen, Princess Maud of Great Britain and Ireland. He was married to the late Queen Martha, Princess of Sweden, who was the daughter of Prince Charles of Sweden and Princess Ingeborg of Denmark; Martha was also the sister of Queen Astrid of Belgium. The king has two daughters and one son, all of whom have married commoners. King Olaf has reigned since 1957.

THE KINGDOM OF HOLLAND

HOUSE OF ORANGE-NASSAU

Her Majesty Juliana, Queen of Holland, Princess of Orange-Nassau

Queen Juliana is sixty-three years old and is the only child of Queen Wilhelmina of Holland and Duke Henry of Mecklenburg. She married Prince Bernard of Lippe-Biesterfeld, the son of Prince Bernard of Lippe-Biesterfeld and the Baroness Armgard of Siestoroff-Cramm. The queen and Prince Bernard have four daughters. Princess Beatrice is married to Claus von Amsberg, now prince of Holland; Princess Irene is married to Prince Hugh de Bourbon-Parma, son of Prince Xavier de Bourbon-Parma and Madeleine de Bourbon-Busset; Princess Margriet is married to Peter van Vollenhoven of Holland; and Princess Marie-Christine is not married. Juliana has reigned since 1948.

THE KINGDOM OF SWEDEN

HOUSE OF BERNADOTTE
His Majesty King Gustaf VI Adolph, King of Sweden

King Gustaf is ninety years old and is the son of King Gustaf V and Princess Victoria of Bade. He was first married to the late Princess Marguerite of Great Britain and Ireland, who was the daughter of Prince Arthur of Great Britain and Ireland, the duke of Connaught, and of Princess Louise-Marguerite of Prussia. She died in May, 1920. Secondly, he married Lady Mountbatten, Princess Louise of Battenberg, the daughter of Lord Mountbatten and Princess Victoria of Hess. The king and his first queen produced five children. The eldest, Prince Gustaf-Adolph, was killed in an airplane accident in 1947; he was married to Princess Sybille of Saxe-Coburg and Gotha, daughter of the duke of Saxe-Coburg and Gotha, Prince of Great Britain and Ireland, and Princess Victoria-Adelaide of Schleswig-Holstein-Sonderburg-Glucksburg. The late Prince is the father of one son and four daughters, one of whom, Princess Brigitte, is married to Prince Jean-George of Hohenzollern. King Gustaf has reigned since 1950.[2]

NOTES

1. As the galleys of this book were being prepared, the situation of the Greek sovereign changed abruptly. On June 1, 1973, the other shoe dropped for King Constantine of Greece. George Papadopoulos, head of state and Premier since March 1972, announced that the monarchy was abolished, and proclaimed Greece a republic. The Greek people, he said, would be asked later to approve the change, to ratify a new constitution, and to elect a president by referendum.

King Constantine's position, therefore, must be defined as claimant as of mid-1973.

Whatever the eventual outcome, Papadopoulos' announcement has brought chills and shudders to Madrid, Copenhagen, Stockholm, London, and to all places where monarchy exists—in fact or in dreams.

2. On September 15, 1973, King Gustaf died and was succeeded by his grandson who became, upon his installation (not coronation), King Carl XVI Gustaf of Sweden—the world's youngest monarch succeeding the world's oldest monarch. King Carl Gustaf (twenty-seven) is unmarried.

APPENDIX D   *Dukes, Princes, Grandees, and Peers*

The amateur royalty-watcher who becomes involved to the point of meeting them, dining in the same houses, generally *caring*, should be alerted to a pitfall—or, at least to possible oversights. Aside from such immediately recognizable names as Habsburg, Bourbon, Romanoff, Savoy, Hohenzollern, Marlborough, and so on, there are many other names that flourish and have royal, princely, ducal, and historic as well as current pertinence to the watcher. As a guide for the devoted amateur, here are some names by some countries that should cause the pulse to throb upon the hearing. The amateur watcher should be able to recognize these names immediately; there is no need to be selective or discretionary, to be able to tell the *real* ones from the *others*. That ability comes only to the professionals.

As the ears become attuned to these names, it should be remembered that their identification with the country does not confine them there. If anything, these names are ubiquitous—many necessarily so, as in the case of the Poles and the Russians:

BELGIUM (DUKES AND PRINCES)

Arenberg	Ligne	Riquet de Caraman-Chi-
Bernadotte	Looz-Corswarem	may
Bethune-Hesdigneul	Merode	Ursel
Croy		Wellington

SPAIN (DUKES AND GRANDEES)

Albaida	Aycinema	Casa Enrile
Alcanices	Bejar	Casa-Gijon
Almendares	Benameji	Casa Real
Arecibo	Caceres	Castelar
Arion	Campo Real	Castrillo
Astorga	Cardona	Cerralbo
Atrisco	Casa Calderon	Cheste

Chinchon
Cienfuegos
Cifuentes
Cuba
Escalona
Ezpeleta de Veire
Fèrnan-Nunez
Floridablanca
Frias
Gavia
Guad El Jesu
Guadalcazar
Guaqui
L'Infantado
La Alcudia
La Casa de Lazcano Valmediano
La Conquista
La Habana
La Hornachuelos
La Mina

La Puebla de los Valles
La Romano
La Torrecilla
Los Castillejos
Mancera
Medina Sidonia
Miraflores
Moctezuma
Modica
Molins
Monterrey
Montijo
Mora
Motrico
Najera
Onate
Osuna
Penalver
Penaranda de Bracamonte
Perales del Rio
Pinohermoso

Prim
Rivas
Roncali
Salinas de Rio Pisuerga
San Carlos
San Fernando
San Marcos
Santa Colombo
Santa Cruz de Mudela
Sastago
Selva Alegre
Siruela
Sotomayor
Superunda
Torrejon
Torres-Cabrera
Uceda
Valle de Oaxana
Veragua
Villagonzalo
Vistahermosa

FRANCE (DUKES AND PRINCES)

Abrantes
Albufera
Antibes
Arenberg
Audiffret-Pasquier
Auerstaedt
Ayen
Bassano
Bauffremont
Beauvau
Beuvron
Bidache
Bissacia
Blacas
Brissac
Broglie
Cadore
Caraman
Des Cars
Castries
Caylus
Chalais
Chaulnes et Picquigny
Clermont-Tonnerre
Croy
Dalmatie
Decazes
Doudeauville
Duras-Chatellux

Elchingen
Essling
Estissac
Faucigny-Lucinge
Feltre
Fezensac
Fitz-James
Gramont
Guiche
Harcourt
La Force
La Moskowa
La Rochefoucauld
La Roche-Guyon
La Tour D'Auvergne Lauraguais
La Tremoille
Lesparre
Levis Mirepoix
Liancourt
Lorge
Luynes et Chevreuse
Magenta
Maille
Martigues
Marmier
Massa di Carrara
Montebello
Montmorency

Mortemart
Mouchy
Murat
Noailles
Orange
Otrante
Pozzo di Borgo
Poix
Polignac
Praslin
Rarecourt de la Vallec de Pimodan
Rauzan
Ravese
Reggio
Richelieu
Rivoli
Robech
Rohan
Sabran
San Lorenzo
Talleyrand
Tascher de la Pagerie
Umbriano del Precetto
Uzes
Valencay
Vandieres
Wagram
Yvetot

GREAT BRITAIN (DUKES AND PEERS)

Abercorn
Argyll
Atholl
Beaufort
Bedford
Buccleuch and Queens-
berry
Devonshire
Fife
Grafton

Hamilton
Leeds
Leinster
Manchester
Marlborough
Montrose
Mountbatten
Newcastle
Norfolk
Northumberland

Portland
Richmond and Gordon
Roxburghe
Rutland
Saint-Albans
Somerset
Sutherland
Wellington
Westminster

ITALY (DUKES AND PRINCES)

Acquaviva d'Aragona
Alliata
Aldobrandini
Antici-Mattei
Archinto
Barberini
Boncompagni
Borghese
Caffarelli
Caracciolo di Cellamare
Caracciolo Pisquizi
Caracciolo Rosso
Caramanico
Carrego Bertolini
Cattareo della Volta
Colonna
Corsini
del Drago
Ferrero
Gaetani
Goetani dell' Aquila
Gallarati-Scotti
Ginori Conti
Guistiniani
Gonzague

Guasco Gallarati
Lancellotti
Lante Montefeltre della
Rovere
Lanza
Lodi
Lucchesi-Polli
Maresca
Marescotti
Massino
Massino Lancellotti
Medicis
Meli-Lupi
Monroy
Morra
di Napoli
Odescalchi
Orsini
Ottoboni
Pallavicini
Paterno di Biscari
Paterno di Carcaci
Paterno di Sperlinga
Patrizi
Pico de la Mirandola

Pio di Savoia
Premuda
Proto
Rospigliosi
Rossi di Montelera
Ruffo
Ruffo di Calabria
Saint-Bar
Saluzzo
Salviati
San Faustino
San Felice
de Sangro
Serra
Sforza-Cesarini
di Somma
Soragna
Spadafora
Strozzi
Torelli
Torlonia
Valsavoia
Vergara Caffarelli
Visconti

POLAND (PRINCES)

Czartoryski
Czetwertynski
Gedroic
Jablonowski
Lubecki
Lubomirski

Massalski
Oginski
Ossolinski
Poniatowski
Poninski
Puzyna de Kozielski

Radziwill
Sangusko
Sapieha
Sulkowski
Woroniecki
Zajaczek

PORTUGAL (DUKES)

Cadaval
Lafoes
Loule

Miranda do Corvo
Palmela

Saldanha
Vitoria

RUSSIA AND GEORGIA (PRINCES)

Abachidze
Amilakhivari
Andronikov
Antchabodze
Bagration-Moukhransky
Barclay de Tolly-Wey-
    marn
Bariatinsky
Belosselsky
Cantacuzene
Chalikov
Chelechpansky
Dachkov
Dadeschkeliani
Dadiani
Dolgoroukoff
Engalytcheff
Eristoff
Eristoff de Ratcha
Gagarine
Galitzine
Gortchakov
Gourielli

Inalipa
Khilokov
Khovansky
Kossatkine-Rostovsky
Kotschoubey
Kourakine
Kropotkine
Lobanow-Rostovsky
Lopoukhine
Lvov
Makaeff
Massalsky
Menchikov
Mingrelie
Nakaschidze
Obolensky
Odoevsky
Orbeliani
Oukhtomisky
Ouroussov
Paskewitch-Erivansky
Poutiatine

Prozorovsky
Repnine-Volkorsky
Rjevsky
Saltykov
Schakhowskoy-Glebow-
    Strechnew
Schervaschidze
Stcherbatov
Tatistcheff
Tchavtchavadze
Tcherkassky
Tchkneidze
Tchkotoua
Tchkotoua de Tchkonia
Tcholokaeff
Toumanoff
Troubetzkoy
Tsitsianov
Vatchnadze
Viazemsky
Volkonsky
Youssoupoff

GERMANY AND AUSTRIA-HUNGARY (PRINCES)

Anhalt
Arenberg
Aspremont
Auersberg
Bade
Bassenheim
Bentheim
Berg
Birckenfeld
Brunswick
Castell
Colloredo-Mansfield
Dietrichstein
Erbach
Erpach
Esterhazy de Galantha
Freyberg
Fugger
Furstenberg
Giech
Graevenitz
Graffen-Egg
Hanau
Hatzfeldt
Hesse
Hohen-Ems

Hohenlohe
Hohen-Waldeck
Hohnzollern
Holstein
Isemburg
Kaunitz
Kinsky
Kirchberg
Koenigseck
La Marck
Lamberg
Leiningen
Leiningen-Dabsburg
Leiningen-Westerburg
Liechtenstein
Limburg-Stirum
Lippe
Lolkowicz
Lowenstein-Wertheim
Manderscheid
Mecklemburg
Merode
Metternich
Montfort
Nassau
Neipperb

Nesselrode
Nostitz
Oettingen
Oldenburg
Ortenburg
Ost-Frise
Pappenheim
Piccolomini
Platen
Platen-Hallermund
Porcia
Puckler und Limpourb
Quadt-Wykradt-Isny
Rantzau
Rechberg
Rechteren Limburg
Reussen de Plauen
Rosenberg
Salm
Salm et Reifferscheidt
Saxe
Saxe-Lauenburg
Sayn und Wittgenstein
Schlick
Schonborn
Schonburg

Schwartzburg	Thurn und Taxis	Wartenberg
Schwarzenberg	Traun	Weissenwolff
Sintzendorff	Trautmansdorf	Wied
Solms	Trautson	Wild und Rhingrave
Stadion	Vehlen	Windisch-Graetz
Starhemberg	Waldburg	Wolffstein
Stolberg	Waldeck	Wurmbrand-Stuppach
Sultzbach	Waldstein	Wurtemberg

One should not despair if the name of a favorite count or baron is not on the lists. It may merely mean that he is not a duke, prince, peer, or grandee. Even in royal and noble circles there must be more Indians than chiefs. It is also possible that he is related to the above families. The practiced royalty-watcher soon learns a rudimentary complexity: The obvious ranking of titles per se—king, duke, prince, count, baron, viscount, marquis, and so on—does not necessarily indicate the intrinsic "rank" of the bearer. For example, the Count of Paris and the Count of Barcelona carry immeasurably more heraldic clout than a Prince Troubetskoy or a Duke di San Miniato. And many of the personages carry a number of titles.

APPENDIX E *Historical Order of Antiquity of the Royal Houses of Europe*

While many of the noble and royal families are more ancient, the official antiquity of the house is judged from the date the empire, kingdom, or duchy became a recognized or accepted national entity.

1) France (481)
2) Spain (718)
3) England (828)
4) Poland (963)
5) Hungary (1001)
6) Ireland (1002)
7) Denmark (1015)
8) Bohemia (1088)
9) Two Sicilies (1130)
10) Sweden (1132)
11) Portugal (1139)
12) Prussia (1701)
13) Sardinia (1720)
14) Russia (1721)

15) Bavaria (1805)
16) Saxony (Dec. 11, 1806)
17) Württemberg (Dec. 26, 1806)
18) Hanover (1814)
19) Netherlands (1816)
20) Belgium (1831)
21) Greece (1832)
22) Turkey (1856)
23) Italy (1860)
24) Serbia (March 6, 1881)
25) Rumania (March 14, 1881)
26) Norway (1905)
27) Bulgaria (1908)
28) Albania (1928)

APPENDIX F   *The American Monarchial Connection*

It sometimes tickles the secret fancies of latent American monarchists to savor the fact that Queen Elizabeth II and George Washington are directly related. Washington's great-grandfather, Colonel Augustine Warner of Virginia, was also Elizabeth's great-great-great-great-great-great-great-great-grandfather:

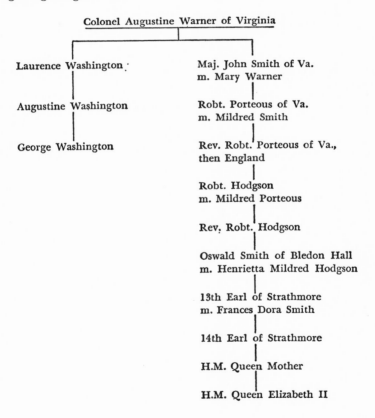

Colonel Augustine Warner of Virginia

Laurence Washington

Augustine Washington

George Washington

Maj. John Smith of Va.
m. Mary Warner

Robt. Porteous of Va.
m. Mildred Smith

Rev. Robt. Porteous of Va.,
then England

Robt. Hodgson
m. Mildred Porteous

Rev. Robt. Hodgson

Oswald Smith of Bledon Hall
m. Henrietta Mildred Hodgson

13th Earl of Strathmore
m. Frances Dora Smith

14th Earl of Strathmore

H.M. Queen Mother

H.M. Queen Elizabeth II

APPENDIX G   *Ten Points of Counsel for Serious Royalty-Watchers*

1) Know that there are *nine reigning* European royal families.
2) Know that there are valid *claimants* to the thrones of *fourteen* existing European countries.
3) Subscribe to the bi-monthly publication, *The Monarchist, The Journal of the Monarchist League,* Lt. Col. J. C. du Parc Braham, 29 York Street, London, W1. It covers every possible aspect of monarchy in all parts of the world: social notes, obituaries, book reviews, correspondence, histories, essays, political commentaries. For the truly addicted, it is the best possible bargain at twenty-five cents per copy.
4) Buy: *Le Petit Gotha Illustré* by Armand Chaffanjon, Editions SERG, Paris. It was first published in 1968 and will be updated every few years. This book—which costs about $25—is a sort of pocket reference book of royal European genealogy and heraldry.
5) *Burke's Peerage,* edited by Peter Townend, London, is another prerequisite for the serious watcher who is particularly drawn to the British personages and their relatives.
6) Do not slight one royal family for another. They are mostly all closely related.
7) Know the family names of various members of the royal houses. There are many big ones that you have never heard of.
8) Do not talk religion too seriously. Almost all the royals are relatives, and the religious lines—unlike those of most commoners— cross each other without prejudice whether Roman Catholic, Anglican, Lutheran, Greek Orthodox, Eastern Orthodox, Russian Orthodox, or Dutch Reformed. The only non-Christian claimants

are King Leka of Albania and Prince Osman Fuad of Turkey who are Moslems.

9) Remember that royal persons are not Gothic aliens in a new age. They are well-informed, broadly cultured people. They are not fools, but can easily recognize one.

10) Do not try to marry one: You may end up with more problems than you guessed—including hemophilia. And unless you have some very old and very blue blood in your own veins, it could be an irritating courtship.

APPENDIX H *The Relationships Between the Reigning Sovereigns of Europe*
(AS OF MAY, 1973)

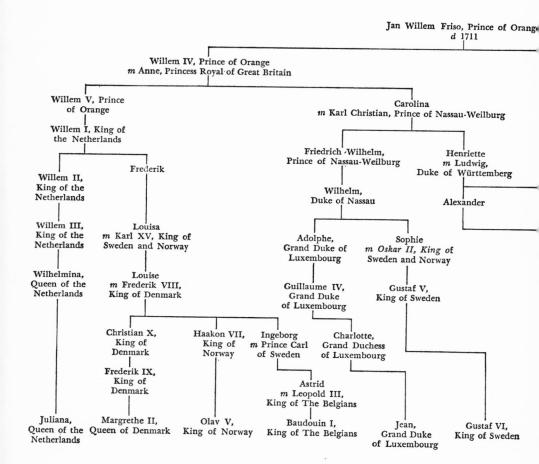

Bibliography

BIBLIOGRAPHY

Alexandra, Queen of Yugoslavia. *For Love of a King*. New York: Doubleday & Company, 1956.

Aronson, Theo. *The Coburgs of Belgium*. London: Cassell & Company, 1969.

Bennett, Daphne. *Vicky*. London: Wm. Collins Sons & Co., 1972.

Bergamini, John. *The Tragic Dynasty*. London: Constable & Company, 1971.

Boulanger, Robert. *Turkey*. Paris: Hachette, 1970.

Chauvire, Roger. *History of Ireland*. London: Burns, Oates and Washbourne, 1952.

Chiffanjon, Arnaud. *Le Petit Gotha Illustré*. Paris: Editions Serg, 1968.

Coutant de Saisseval, Guy. *Maisons Imperiales et Royales d'Europe*. Paris: Editions du Palais-Royal, 1966.

Curtis, Edmund. *History of Ireland*. London: Methuen & Co., 1936.

Crankshaw, Edward. *The Habsburgs*. London: Wiendenfeld & Nicholson, 1972.

d'Hauterive, Borel. *Annuaire de la Noblesse de France et d'Europe*. Paris: Morant and d'Angerville, 1960.

Fattorusso, J. *Kings and Queens of England and France*. Florence: Medici Historical Atlases, 1954.

Foran de Saint-Bar, Thomas. *Portrait d'un Roi*. Paris: Editions Serg, 1968.

Frederica, Queen of The Hellenes. *A Measure of Understanding*. London: Macmillan & Co., 1971.

Knupffer, George and James Page. *King Simeon II of the Bulgarians*. Kings of Tomorrow Series, No. 2. London: Monarchist Press, 1969.

MacLysaght, Edward. *Irish Families*. Dublin: Hodges & Figgs, 1968.

Mestas, Alberto de. *Souverains et Pretendants en 1964*. Paris: Les Cahiers Nobles, 1964.

Miller-Brown, Conrad. *The Queen and Her Royal Relations*. London: Rupert Hart-Davis, 1953.

O'Hart. *Irish Pedigrees*. London: McClasban & Gill, 1876.

O'Neill, Terence. *Autobiography of Terence O'Neill*. London: Hart-Davis, 1972.

Petrie, Sir Charles. *King Charles III of Spain.* New York: John Day Company, Inc., 1971.

Poole, S. B. and R. Poole. *Royal Mysteries and Pretenders.* London: Blandford Press, 1969.

Stewart, Desmond. *Turkey.* New York: Time Inc., 1965.

Townend, Peter, ed. *Burke's Peerage Ltd.* London: 1969.

Valko, W. G. *Who's Who in Reigning Royalty.* Philadelphia: Community Press, 1970.

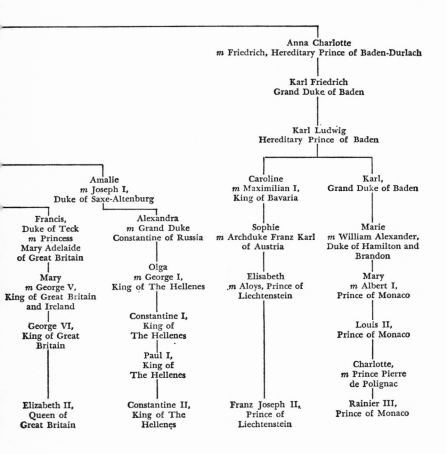

Anna Charlotte
m Friedrich, Hereditary Prince of Baden-Durlach

Karl Friedrich
Grand Duke of Baden

Karl Ludwig
Hereditary Prince of Baden

Amalie
m Joseph I,
Duke of Saxe-Altenburg

Caroline
m Maximilian I,
King of Bavaria

Karl,
Grand Duke of Baden

Francis,
Duke of Teck
m Princess
Mary Adelaide
of Great Britain

Alexandra
m Grand Duke
Constantine of Russia

Sophie
m Archduke Franz Karl
of Austria

Marie
m William Alexander,
Duke of Hamilton and
Brandon

Mary
m George V,
King of Great Britain
and Ireland

Olga
m George I,
King of The Hellenes

Elisabeth
m Aloys, Prince of
Liechtenstein

Mary
m Albert I,
Prince of Monaco

George VI,
King of Great
Britain

Constantine I,
King of
The Hellenes

Louis II,
Prince of Monaco

Paul I,
King of
The Hellenes

Charlotte,
m Prince Pierre
de Polignac

Elizabeth II,
Queen of
Great Britain

Constantine II,
King of The
Hellenes

Franz Joseph II,
Prince of
Liechtenstein

Rainier III,
Prince of Monaco